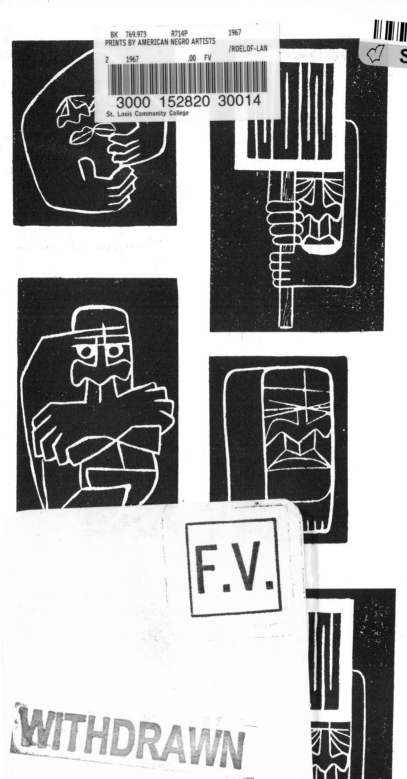

PRINTS BY AMERICAN NEGRO ARTISTS
PUBLISHED BY CULTURAL EXCHANGE CENTER
OF LOS ANGELES, CALIFORNIA
ROSEMARIE VON STUDNITZ, PRESIDENT
EDITED BY T.V.ROELOF-LANNER, PH.D.

PRINTS BY AMERICAN NEGRO ARTISTS

COPYRIGHT 1965
BY CULTURAL EXCHANGE CENTER
OF LOS ANGELES, CALIFORNIA
PRINTED IN THE UNITED STATES OF AMERICA
LIBRARY OF CONGRESS CATALOG CARD NUMBER 65-24998

COPYRIGHT 1967
BY CULTURAL EXCHANGE CENTER
OF LOS ANGELES, CALIFORNIA
PRINTED IN THE UNITED STATES OF AMERICA
LIBRARY OF CONGRESS CATALOG CARD NUMBER 67-16123

VOLUME ONE OF THE SERIES
"CONTEMPORARY AMERICAN ARTISTS"

PRINTS

BY
AMERICAN NEGRO
ARTISTS

SECOND EDITION

CULTURAL EXCHANGE CENTER
OF LOS ANGELES - CALIFORNIA

TABLE OF CONTENTS

FOREWORD
FIRST EDITION

The "CULTURAL EXCHANGE CENTER" of Los Angeles has made in its publications and its exhibits mostly territorial distinctions in order to promote understanding and inspiration of the Art Worlds of the United States and Europe. The fact that in the publication "PRINTS BY AMERICAN NEGRO ARTISTS", racial distinction is being made, needs an explanation. The showing of prints exclusively by American Negro Artists has two reasons. The great public is not aware that the Negro minority in America produces artists of great stature and that the American Negro Artists are reaching for the stars exactly like their white brothers. The second reason is rather from the viewpoint of the art critic who likes to investigate, which forces and which ideas are inspiring the American Negro Artists. Can one still recognize traces of the African ancestry? Does one find manifestions of the Negro Rights Movement? Or can one not distinguish between the artistic trends of the American Negro and the Caucasian Artists in many cases?

The production of this publication was in the able hands of Dr. T.V. Roelof-Lanner, the editor of this book. His approach to the reproduction of the pictures is unconventional. Publishers of Art Books use normally the four-color-process, which is a photomechanical way of reproduction. This may do for the reproduction of oil paintings, but certainly not for the reproduction of color woodcuts. In order to get a close image of the original, color-separation by hand is essential. In fact for the reproduction of many of the prints, new methods had to be found and the individual treatment and the individual printing of the pictures give the book "PRINTS BY AMERICAN NEGRO ARTISTS" its unique flavor.

Too many people gave a helping hand during the production of this book to be mentioned individually. CULTURAL EXCHANGE CENTER appreciates their efforts and expresses sincerest thanks.

One person has to be singled out and given the highest praise for her outstanding cooperation with the editor: This is Mrs. Ruth G. Waddy. Ruth Waddy is closely connected with the Art Life in Los Angeles. She made herself a name as a creative artist and was elected president of the artists group "ART-WEST". She also has excellent connection to artists all over the United States and volunteered to make personal contact with the contributing artists. Her efforts have been highly successful. Ruth Waddy expresses her artistic view-point in an interesting introduction which she wrote for "PRINTS BY AMERICAN NEGRO ARTISTS".

I hope sincerely that CULTURAL EXCHANGE CENTER has rendered a valuable public service by presenting the work of the Young American Negro Artists in the publication:

"PRINTS BY AMERICAN NEGRO ARTISTS"

ROSEMARIE VON STUDNITZ
(President of Cultural Exchange Center)

FOREWORD
second edition

The book "PRINTS BY AMERICAN NEGRO ARTISTS" was so enthusiastically received that it encouraged CULTURAL EXCHANGE CENTER to prepare a second greatly enlarged edition. A number of pictures by outstanding artists have been added and exhaustive informations about the contributing artists included. Some of the artists state their artistic creed and outline their philosophy pertaining life and environments. The most important factor is undoubtedly the excellent article "One hundred-fifty years of Afro-American Art" by Prof. Dr. James A. Porter at Howard University, Washington, D.C. This essay sets the publication "Prints by American Negro Artists" firmly into the framework of historical development and shows how the oeuvre of Negro Artists is an integral part of American culture.

"PRINTS BY AMERICAN NEGRO ARTISTS" is the Number I of a series of books on Contemporary American Art which Cultural Exchange Center plans to publish in the near future. Number II "PAINTINGS AND SCULPTURE BY AMERICAN NEGRO ARTISTS", and Number III "CONTEMPORARY AMERICAN ARTISTS IN AMERICAN MUSEUMS" are already in preparation. The latter will show to the world the scope of Art-Activities in the Present-Day United States and guide the American public to the art-treasures of its own nation.

ROSEMARIE VON STUDNITZ
(President of Cultural Exchange Center)

ONE HUNDRED-FIFTY YEARS OF AFRO-AMERICAN ART

Scientific research in this country has contributed invaluable evidence for the prolongation of African culture into the complex civilizations of the Western Hemisphere. If just prior to World War I, much of the world may still have regarded the American Negro as a rather unpromising graft upon the tree of American civilization, there is not now, nor has there been for more than two generations, any defensible reason whatever, for persistence in that belief. Informed by objective studies of the breadth, complexity, and stratified depth of western life and culture, and cognizant of its ethnic and cultural diversity, the unprejudiced may happily accept that cultural heritage of the American Negro in which African characteristics predominate.

Prior to World I, there were but few white students of American culture or of the cultural potential of different social and ethnic groups in America who possessed a thorough knowledge of Negro life and culture. Per contra, there were such enlightened anthropologists and masters of objective historical method as Franz Boas, the historian Albert Bushnell Hart, and sociologists like the late W. E. B. DuBois whose writings lifted the scales from the eyes of all who were willing to read them believingly. Indeed, one wonders if our present disposition to weigh the desserts of the Negro in the light of a more perfect knowledge of his past could ever have been developed without the intellectual or scholarly and sometimes programmatic leadership of such great Americans as W. E. B. DuBois, Carter G. Woodson, Kelly Miller, Alain LeRoy Locke and the late E. Franklin Frazier.

It would be non-sensical to claim that the broadening appreciation of the Negro and his arts in the Western Hemisphere was entirely due to the activity of Negro scholarship or connoisseurship. As a matter of fact, the Negro scholar has often been supported in that connection by the cooperative as well as the collaborative assistance of white intellectuals who were sincerely enthusiastic to correct the record and to reveal the truth. For example, the sympathetic and constructive work of scholars like the late anthropologist Melville J. Herskovits, and the ethnographers Morton Kahn and Leyburn, has brilliantly complemented the writings of Rayford Logan, Alain Locke and Lorenzo D. Turner who focused attention upon the persistent,—as opposed to the latent—"africanisms" in the culture of the southern United States, the Caribbean, and the several Guianas of South America, thus projecting a new realm of discourse and attracting further scholarly effort to the interpretation of Afro-American cultures. It will also be recalled that the tardiness of white America to acknowledge wholeheartedly the Negro's contribution to popular music and especially to Jazz was first dealt a serious thrust by the knowledgeable published writings of European lovers of Jazz. In addition, Anton Dvorak's "New World Symphony" and Henry Krehbiel's Afro-American Folk-Songs provided even the somewhat skeptical American Negro with sound reasons for accepting the Negro Spiritual as an art form.

With the advent of the "New Negro Movement" in the 1920's, the formative arts of painting, sculpture, of the print and of design finally became the acknowledged province of the American Negro. Prior to that period, the impact of African art, as developed through the conscious use made of its idiom by Picasso, Matisse, Vlaminck, Derain and certain German Expressionist painters, had also been felt in the Americas. Yet, the significance of that event for Negro art in America was not defined until Alain Locke employed his astute critical powers and his ready pen to appraise the past performances of the Negro artist and to explain the Afro-American's connection with African art as "The Ancestral Arts." Perhaps it is now quite certain that Locke's main contribution to our appreciation of modern "Afro-American art" was his interesting apology for the distinctive aesthetico-racial (but not the "primitive"), traits of African art; and second, his rather romantic advocacy of those characteristics as a point of departure for the young American Negro artist.

It is important to realize that evidence of African survivals in the earliest manifestations of Afro-American creativity in the United States demonstrably exists. The writer of this essay, in his book Modern Negro Art, published in 1943, devotes an entire chapter to supporting evidence of the conscious survival of African art forms and techniques in some parts of the Southern United States, notably in the States of Alabama, Louisiana, North and South Carolina, and Virginia. Architecture offers proofs of this cultural phenomenon in techniques of house construction and the making of wrought-iron supports and ornaments for balconies and porches in New Orleans, Louisiana, Alabama, Charleston, South Carolina and parts of Virginia. The crafts of weaving, wood carving and embroidery also allow us to discern the retention of African features; and Cedric Dover in his American Negro Art illustrates an interesting type of "plantation pottery" produced by slave craftsmen of North and South Carolina that bears unmistakable signs of African recollection in peculiarities of surface design.

Related to these outcroppings, is the fact that countless Negroes were engaged in earning money to buy their freedom through skilled employment as sign painters, silver smiths, as cabinet or as coach-makers, stucco ornamentalists, and, somewhat unexpectedly, as shipwrights. There was even a very early Negro sculptor—Eugene Warbourg of New Orleans—whose principal work until he left New Orleans for the opportunity of study in Europe was the making of ornamental gravestones. To these we must add the early Negro portrait limners, and those Negro sailors as well whose contributions to the immense sum of "scrimshaw art" now to be seen in America's marine museums, must forever remain anonymous and unassigned.

Though the slave were ever so talented, it was rarely artistic talent, but rather painfully acquired mechanical skills, unremitting labor, and, occasionally, thrift, which helped him most to buy his freedom. In general, the slavocracy brutally suppressed, wherever possible, all philanthropic effort to educate the slave. For this and other reasons the Negro rarely emerged in ante-bellum days as an individual artist or even as a privileged, self-employing artisan from the welter of southern industrial strivings.

Even in the North, where opportunities for the talented Negro were more frequent, and repression of the Negro probably less severe, the traces of poverty and the shadow of repression tied the hopes of Negro art to an uncertain future: Such harsh and unfavorable social conditions were the very cause of the scarcity of production attributable to the early talented Negro. It is reasonable to suppose that the same set of social conditions made it inevitable that the majority of Negro artists should ape the residual European art techniques or modes of painting which underlay the American system of art practice and art apprenticeship of that time.

Such inimical influences were transcended, however, in the life and work of a handful of "free" Negroes among whom Patrick Reason, the draftsman-engraver, Robert S. Duncanson, the landscape and mural painter of Cincinnati, the excellent portrait painter, William Simpson, and E. M. Bannister, a painter of naturalistic landscapes and a founding member of the Providence Art Club were plainly the most outstanding artists. Though seemingly unsophisticated in aesthetics, these artists often produced work of a beguiling unpretentiousness which lacked neither dignity nor grace. And there were others,—all free men of the ante-bellum period—among whom I would name the portrait and landscape painter, David Bowser and the Negro Quaker, Robert Douglass, Jr., both of Philadelphia, and Joshua Johnston of Baltimore, a painter of prim portraits, who still remains a somewhat shadowy figure.

The career of Edmonia Lewis, the first Negro woman sculptor, begun prior to the Civil War, came to an end near the turn of the century. While the actual date of her death is not yet known, the many interesting details of her life and work which was known testify to a wonderfully courageous spirit. Her career was a steady and arduous climb to a place of honor and high reputation in Europe and finally in America as one of the foremost American exponents of the neo-classic style in sculpture.

Negro America was largely ignorant of such brief professional triumphs over prejudice and discrimination, since but few Negroes in the last quarter of the nineteenth century could have appreciated the gigantic labors that went into the making of Edmonia Lewis' success as an expatriate American sculptress. And few were aware that Bannister, a "Negro import" from Nova Scotia, had been challenged to become an artist in order to disprove the published assertion that while the Negro obviously possessed an appreciation for art, he had not yet shown a capacity to produce art.

Worthy successors of these early artists appeared in the last quarter of the century: They were Henry Ossawa Tanner, William A. Harper and Meta Warrick Fuller. As an approach to painting, Harper's art illustrates a certain continuity from the work of Bannister. But this analogous relationship vanished rather quickly in the glow and splendor of Harper's landscapes after his adoption of an impressionist technique acquired in France and matured by trips to Mexico and the American West.

Yet no American painter, probably not the great Winslow Homer, nor even the eagle-eyed Thomas Eakins, could match that resplendent vision of a national American culture which had been proposed for them by the poet

Walt Whitman in O Pioneers and in his celebrated political and literary document Democratic Vistas. In fact, only the most gifted among the white American artists of this period were able to escape the deadly dull mechanical routines of portrait painting and banal illustration, or the lofty, remote and classicizing sentiments learned by way of the warmed-over formulas of "beaux-arts" academies in Europe. All such preoccupations were too distant from the basic concerns of the Negro artists to be of any use. And so, turning away from such outworn traditions, the Negro artist wandered perhaps cheerless but alert into the pathless fields of the countryside towards the humble cabins in which he knew that the black freedman, still the backbone of the rural South, could be found and portrayed.

Into such an environment, Henry O. Tanner, during the years when he was still under the influence of his great American teacher, Thomas Eakins, strayed briefly in the 1880's and quickly fashioned therefrom a few fine landscapes and also some spell-binding portrayals of peasant Negroes in which we detect kinship to the sweet though melancholy lyricism that pervades the poetry of Paul Laurence Dunbar. Later, after his self-expatriation to France, Tanner became one of the foremost exponents of the "flight-to-religion" position, seeking in themes of biblical history and faith the broader canvas of human experience and aesthetic emotion.

Meta Vaux Warrick's early sculpture is a hymn to tradition expressed in forms which reflect the intense struggle of a soul with its own nature. In her work, which was clearly inspired by that of Rodin, she occasionally pushed her interpretations of humanity's sad plight to expressional extremes of despair, remorse, anger, and resignation. Certain of these moods were expressed with subtlety, and some awkwardly, but in the main, sincerely. In some ways, she seems to have been a continuator of the earlier Edmonia Lewis, although her brief sojourn in Europe resulted in the acquisition of "impressionist realism" as opposed to her predecessor's neo-classicism.

From 1900 to 1925, Negroes generally had to make their own opportunities in the fine arts. Aware of but little artistic tradition within the race and lacking a clear understanding of the issues confronting American art, Negro talent was forced to seek training or at least guidance in the schools and studios of reputable white artists who would accept them. Often, they were forced to beg for opportunities to study art in a serious way or to exhibit their work. Those who wished to exhibit their work usually had access only to the social rooms of churches, the vestibules and reading rooms of public libraries and Y. M. C. A. buildings, or to the classrooms of Negro public schools. Very little help came to them even through channels of race leadership or education, or from white patrons of means. Discouraging also, was the fact that but few knowledgeable interpreters of Negro art could be found among that day's Negro intellectuals. Apparently more concerned with the general problems of the Negro, race leaders did not too directly or seriously lend support to Negro art or the artist.

Despite such vicissitudes this—the transitional period—produced the first group of "realist" painters and sculptors around 1915. Unable to support themselves by art alone, they were, despite that handicap, keen, if hindered observers of the realities around them. John Henry Adams, Jr., Lenwood Morris, W. O. Thompson, William E. Scott, T. E. Hunster, Edward Harleston, Laura Wheeler Waring and Alan Freelon won praise for their interpretations of Negro character, life and landscape. None of them was a great artist, yet each did achieve results in some way comparable to the work of their better-known white contemporaries of the realist school, who had become derisively distinguished in the public mind by the sobriquet, "The Ashcan School" of painters.

The isolation of the American Negro artist of the transitional period from the mainstream of culture is further illustrated by the fact that the great New York Armory Show of 1913 made little impression on Negro art until the late 1920's. For fully fifteen years after its closing, Negro artists were still preoccupied with academic realism or with a belated impressionism of manner, while all around them new "experimental" ideas derived from European example were divesting American art of a deadly complacency.

Unemployment, labor strikes, mad housing and racial conflict in the larger American cities throughout the 1920's were a consequence of industrial and social dislocations brought on by the first World War. This social upheaval portended the Great Depression of the 1930's. Out of the effort to interpret and probably to exploit such mass disturbances and shifting economic conditions as they affected the Negro was born the intellectual and cultural ferment known as the "New Negro Movement." Then for the first time in history was world attention focused on the cultural heritage and the living arts of the American Negro. An important book that took note of the Negro's achievements in art up to 1925 also pointed out ways in which he might go further. This was The New Negro: An Interpretation, edited by Alain LeRoy Locke.

The careful reader of that book will note that at least a few Negro artists had survived the rough artistic weather of the earlier decades; that indeed, their lack of popularity had been a test of their power of survival. The older artists of that period were Henry O. Tanner, May Howard Jackson, Harleston, Freelon, and Laura Wheeler Waring. Tanner, Meta W. Fuller, and May Howard Jackson were mentioned in Locke's book. They were mentioned critically but not by any means with dispraise. Their work was viewed, however, as representative of an earlier day, but not of the new day. This must be carefully borne in mind if we are to understand the nature of that artistic resurgence which marked Negro culture in the third decade of this century. May Howard Jackson, who died in 1939, and Malvin Gray Johnson, a most promising talent whose untimely death in 1934 was deeply mourned, were two artists of clear and solid objectives who had not time, however, to realize with equal success all the projects they attempted. In retrospect, the same characteristics of non-fulfillment, mar our appreciation of E. A. Harleston who died in 1931.

Realism would appear to be as likely a part of the Negro heritage of art as any other acknowledged artistic tradition. Indeed, it is also an aspect of

African Negro art, although it has been largely alienated from us through disparagements upon it by those who have made it their purpose to misinterpret or to minimize the double heritage of the conceptual and the real, the abstract and the concrete, the imaginative and the representational which are equally present therein. From black Africa's Middle Ages there has risen to challenge modern art and modern taste one of the world's most vigorous traditions of realistic art. The great bronze life heads and the bold but extra-ordinarily poised creations of Benin and the Congo Bakuba of the fifteenth and later centuries strike us as being an almost direct anticipation of certain masterpieces of baroque sculpture by the eighteenth century Brazilian mulatto sculptor, Aleijadinho, or the powerful modeling of the painter-wood engraver Charles White, whose monumental forms realistically projected in paint inevitably recall the diversified legacy of African realism.

It is a fact of rather curious interest that his older contemporary, Sargent Johnson, one of the original "New Negro" talents, is another notable exponent of the same tradition. Also in line with this substantial tradition is the veteran expressionist painter, Beauford Delaney, "the amazing Beauford" of Henry Miller's unique biographical sketch. Indeed, Charles White's powerful social commentary though often symbolic is further inflected in the varied work of Charles Davis, Eldzier Cortor, and John Wilson, three young artists whose canvasses seem to brood over the slum and ghetto lands of our great northern cities. But it is doubtful that Richmond Barthe's sculpture, particularly of the period 1940 to 1948, could be properly appreciated except in the light of that American "new realism" which enlivens and sometimes spiritualizes not only the work of several American practitioners, —the "white regionalists" of the 1930's and 40's,—but also that potent Mexican realism of the 1920's and 1930's.

By 1933, the dehumanizing effect of cubist principles on form was beginning to modify Negro painting, sculpture and graphic art quite significantly. Zestfully introduced to Americans through the Armory Show, this style had first taken firm root in the paintings of the Americans Max Weber, John Marin, Alfred Maurer, Niles Spencer, and Preston Dickinson. A foretaste of the Negro artist's use of cubist forms had been seen in the book illustrations and earliest formal experiments of Aaron Douglas, James L. Wells, Hale Woodruff, and Malvin Gray Johnson. Its radical contrasts of form hardly affected the normative realism, however, of such sculptors as Barthe and Augusta Savage, unless it can be said that it influenced their work toward better structure as well as economy of design and facture.

One of the sources of Cubism had been African Negro sculpture; and it was the recognition of the importance of this connection by Paul Guillaume and other French critics, and later by Albert Barnes and Alain Locke, which effectually attached the cubism of African forms to the new experimental growth of modern Afro-American art.

It may be that the fructifying influence of African art on modern Afro-American art is not yet spent. Individually and separately, I am sure, there must be a fair number of American artists who still have recourse to its discipline, precisely as there are many American artists who still check their own native primitivism by the timeless traditions of American Indian art and American colonial art: But the earlier morphological transfer of its geometric or crystalline shapes has now declined virtually to zero; while something more important, because more expressional as well as abstract, has replaced it.

Nevertheless, it would be rewarding, if space permitted, to trace the gentle evolution of cubist forms in modern Negro art towards and finally into obstraction through the sculpture of Elizabeth Prophet and Augusta Savage, and of the more youthful Henry Bannarn and John Rhoden, not forgetting, by any means, the gingerly rhythms of William H. Johnson's early expressionist paintings, or the surrealist and abstract qualities in the magical abstractions of Harlan Jackson and Harper Phillips. In the bronzes of Barbara Chase and Richard Hunt one detects similar correlations of cryptic forms with even more esoteric meaning.

Although the productions of certain Afro-American artists may seem to draw upon modalities extracted from the personal experience of race, it is unlikely that "racial" or "traditional abstraction" can be identified as a genre of Afro-American art. We are aware, nevertheless, of a kind of conscious "atavism," deriving from the practice of subjectivized illustration of certain folk-themes used in the work of important North American, Cuban, Venezuelan, Haitian and Brazilian artists of Negro extraction. Emergent as far back as the 1940's this phenomenon has persisted almost to the present. The best or at least the most effective instances are to be observed in the paintings of the great Wilfredo Lam and his pupil, Roberto Diago who died untimely. Occasionally, thes culpture of Ramos-Blanco and Rita Longa, both Cubans, is similarly inspired. Many of the Haitian so-called "primitive" painters, among whom the most interesting are Philome Obin, the late Hector Hippolyte, Louverture Poisson, and Rigaud Benoit, to name but a few, have combined renascent African forms with an intense purity of vision that is quite astonishing.

In the United States, a similar intensity of vision is remarked in the brilliant early gouaches of Jacob Lawrence whose "symbolic narratives" are proclamations of color, or in Horace Pippin's folk-memory paintings which manage to hold their own in juxtaposition to Romare Beardon's earlier compositional essays wrought from aggressively disjunctive forms and raw color. Since 1955, the almost annual visits of Lois M. Jones (Mrs. Pierre-Noel) to the "Magical Island" have resulted in watercolors and oils of enchanting landscapes, and harbor and market scenes with colors tempered to the mercurial moods of the Haitian atmosphere.

It may not be inappropriate to mention here the visits in Africa which a few American Negro artists have made with a double purpose to learn more at first hand about contemporary African art and to gratify the irresistible impulse to view and to record the African scene. Moreover, it is quite conceivable that this kind of activity on the part of the American Negro artists, though primarily intended to capture new themes and render new interpretations, has also helped to strengthen cultural ties between American Negroes and Africans. The first to make such a visit with an avowedly journalistic purpose in mind was Elton Fax, an outstanding New York illustrator. His book, African Vignettes, is the pictorial result of his travels in West Africa.

Next, Dr. John T. Biggers, Head of the Department of Art at Texas Southern University, spent a full year in Africa. Biggers chose to focus his artistic tour on Ghana, a choice that no doubt afforded a better opportunity to achieve both unity and cumulative impact of subject content in his designs. It should be stressed that while some of Dr. Bigger's "painterly" drawings were of great size they were reduced to the compass of a folio volume and published most effectively under the title of Ananse; The Web of Life in West Africa.

Jacob Lawrence has been twice to Africa, the first time accompanying an exhibition of his own paintings in the hope of stimulating a free exchange of ideas with African artists in Nigeria. His second visit in June, 1964, was devoted to a painter's research of the African scene and resulted in a large exhibition of his work at Lagos, Ibadan and New York.

The present writer completed a year-long tour of art-historical research and creative painting in West Africa in August, 1964. In addition to an abundance of notes and photographs on forms of West African and Sudanese architecture, the tour produced a harvest of oil paintings and drawings based on African life and mythology in Nigeria, Ghana, Guinea and elsewhere.

Mural painting and relief sculpture by Negro artists still reflect as previously in the days of the Roosevelt administration and the New Deal, the social and topical viewpoints which were inherent in a now discontinued Government Works program for the Arts. Nevertheless, some significant progress was made by our mural painters through the Federal Arts Projects in the 1940's. Under that program, artists of lesser abilities were sometimes employed to decorate walls along with the best; and private patronage also encouraged many of the younger artists thus limelighted by official recognition. Almost without exception, Negro artists were assigned wall spaces in buildings largely in daily use by Negroes, such as schools, hospitals, libraries and community centers. It must be admitted, however, that this obviously considered location for their work was in the last analysis good for the Negro clientele to whom their objective paintings were directed. It was in this way that underprivileged persons could view good works of art. Often they were inspired as well as instructed thereby.

Thus, the historical paintings of Aaron Douglas and William E. Scott, of Charles Alston,—particularly the latter artist's mural series on cycles of Negro history still to be seen in the Harlem Hospital,—and the several mural panels prepared by Vertis Hayes, Charles White, and Hale Woodruff would, if presented together in one grouping, relate the complete history of the Negro people in the United States. Indeed, with few exceptions, our mural painters of today still choose to work within the racial theme and scope. Between Aaron Douglas' Fisk University Murals and the huge paintings completed by Charles Alston and Woodruff for the Golden State Mutual Life Insurance Company in Los Angeles, or the equally fine productions of Elmer Brown in Cleveland and Charles Stallings at Morgan College in Baltimore, there is scarcely a mural painting that does not have as its main content the episodic portrayal of Negro life and history.

Today, the sincere student of the progress of Afro-American art should not expect to find that it follows a single simplistic tenor. Should that student say to himself at the outset that surely such painters as Horace Pippin and Jacob Lawrence whose simple close-knit harmonies seem to probe the very soul of the Negro must have their Negro followers, he would search in vain to find them. Nor would he discover a continuator of that skillful but genuinely naive talent, Leslie Bolling, whose carvings still delight the purists among American museum directors. The explanation probably lies in the fact that the present titantic struggle for human rights and cultural recognition has made the Negro people indifferent to the child-like, or to the simply lyrical aspects of art.

Indeed, there is a restless dissatisfaction too poignantly symptomatic of growing frustration and anger in the work of many artists to go unnoticed. Though one may wish that some of their efforts at social criticism were even more direct or accusatory, it takes but little probing below what may seem just a smear of color to detect a message of individual protest amid frightening forms of anger and fear. There seems to be much reason to believe that some of the tendencies in Negro art today are responsive to the words of writers like James Baldwin and Leroi Jones, even as yesterday Negro painters were giving symbolic graphic expression to the ideas of Claude McKay and Richard Wright or applying to pictorial themes the somber, yet majestic lament of Eliot's The Wastelands.

Even the less sensitive among us could hardly fail to see that the countless acts and declarations of the struggle for Civil Rights have entered the subjects and the forms of Negro art. Formerly, such painting or sculpture had been regarded as racist propaganda rather than art, and was condemned as an over-dramatization of feelings of separateness in American life or as hyper-sensitiveness to race discrimination. Yet, today the same appalling scenes of the Negro ghetto and the "wastelands" of the American cities are painted masterfully by Hughie Lee-Smith, Charles White, Edward Loper, Charles McGee and Ernest Crichlow, not in the mode of "Pop Art," but in strangely moving orchestrations of color and form. In many instances the effect of their work is that of a prayer and of emotional release instead of despair as one sees in the splendid oils of David Driskell and the apocalyptic subjects of James L. Wells. In truth, such paintings are directional signals to action for those who are competent to understand their symbolic language.

It is inevitable that the American Negro artists' striving for self-expression and for significant interpretation should continue; but it is also to be anticipated that he should not remain indifferent to the shocks and surprises of the social and racial conflicts and upheavals of the day. The path of the present-day Negro is sown with racist mines and booby-traps, and the barbed wire of legal hindrances of this as well as an earlier day. It is interesting, however, and, in the main, wonderfully encouraging to note how the younger Negro artists are facing up to the hysterical challenges and the blatant issues which assail their progress toward full citizenship on every hand.

In New York City, the recently formed Spiral Group is now rising above a somewhat puerile methodology to reach a new group consensus and group solidarity underlying their work as artists and their honorable and independent effort as Americans. In Los Angeles, one is amazed and encouraged to observe with what brilliance of attack and of resolution a group of young Negro and white artists led by Noah Purifoy have demonstrated the possibility of transforming the wasteland of Watts and its despairing aftermath into a programmatic art full of oddly cohesive ideas as well as materials which symbolize the determination to erase the ghettoed existence of all such places as Watts. The impression gained from the fine exhibition of The Negro in American Art recently organized by Frederick S. Wight for the University of California at Los Angeles Art Galleries is that quite a number of the Los Angeles artists belong to the progressive wing of young printmakers, sculptors and painters who are bringing new vitality into Negro art.

Looking at the work of these young artists, one feels that their seeming preference for black and white over color may be in the interest of a clear presentation of aesthetically valid though hard and obdurate truths of observation and experience. Nevertheless, one feels almost irresistibly drawn toward the paintings of Sam Gilliam of Washington, D.C. and Mavis Pusey of Los Angeles whose brilliant, taut lines and planar simplifications may indeed be prophetic anticipations of a new and, hopefully, a more ordered world. And glimpsing the compartmentalized cosmos of Betye Saar's "The Astrologer's Window" or the fractured tonal beauty of Marvin Harden's larva-like "Melancholia No. 25," one feels impelled to ask,—are these songs of despair or apostrophizing odes to a spirit of resignation, or, perhaps, of defiance?

Like Purifoy's "Sir Watts" or Melvin Edward's "A Necessary Angle" these works are an astonishing mixture of the banal and the implausible, and invite comparison with the satirical paintings of the earlier German school of Neue Sachlichkeit. It would be rather depressing, in any case, to believe that like the "sculpture machines" of Rube Goldberg they are merely comic or, perhaps, derisive. Similarly, to appraise them as mere experimentation would be to invite charges of boorish or inept criticism. That they do move us into a world of macabre, sur-realistic dissonance is a tribute to the skillful use of symbolic forms which lie just below the surface of the real.

It is certain that the double standard of appraisal and of employment that formerly discouraged the Negro artist is fast disappearing, especially so when we are able to name quite a significant number of Negro artists who are now teaching in college art departments or in schools of art which only yesterday had exclusively white facilities. In addition to that bit of progress, we note that Negro art patrons are appearing in ever-growing numbers, not just as occasional buyers, but as collectors who often purchase their art directly from art galleries established in such cities as New York, Detroit, Chicago, Washington, D.C., Los Angeles and San Francisco.

Yet it is unlikely that we shall ever have a truly great Afro-American artist among us until American society completely accepts the Negro and his valid interpreters. This wished-for relationship is still far from arriving although it is so much desired by all who love America and hope that she will fulfill the promise of equality. Present social conditions indicate the need to establish a greater cultural purpose in the heart of this nation. This must be accomplished not merely for the sake of culture but for peace and human salvation. The present militancy of the Negro relative to this necessity has been interpreted as the actual conscience of America pricking her towards goals of social justice and moral action. To question the validity of such a viewpoint is to contemplate anew the present significance of American Negro art.

I conclude in the conviction that the American Negro is now moving with the great wave of creativity which is cresting in America. This, in fact, is a cultural upsurge of crucial importance, and it offers the artist and the writer unprecedented opportunities for the development of mobility and independence of creative thought and imagery. The question is will the Negro artist continue to exploit his present opportunities in the realization that such an engagement is more than a test of sheer tenacity? It is a challenge to his whole capability, even though the answer to the query actually rests with the Negro people and not, specifically, with their interpreters. Therefore, it is predictable that only the as yet unspent social and cultural drives of that people can unfailingly sustain the Afro-American artist as he embraces the broader opportunities of the future.

JAMES A. PORTER

PART TWO

LiST OF piCTURES

AMOS, EMMA: "HARVEST II" - Color Etching

ARNOLD, RALPH: "UNTITLED" - Color Lithograph

BIGGERS, JOHN T.: "BROKEN STONE" - Lithograph

BRANDON, BRUMSIC Jr.: Title Page, Jacket, and Fly Leaves: "SIT IN" - "THE NON VIOLENT" - "THE MARCH" "PICKET" - "MOURNING THE MARTYRED" - "THE MILITANT" - Woodcuts

BRITTON, S.: "UNTITLED" - Woodcut

BURNETT, CALVIN: "THREE CRIPPLED DRUNKS" - Serigraph

BURROUGHS, MARGARET: "ABSTRACTION" - Linocut

CADOO, JOYCE: "DECLINE AND FALL" - Color Woodcut

CAREY, MEL: "HUNGER" - Scratch Board

CARTER, YVONNE: "LATERAL MOVEMENT" - Etching

CHELTENHAM, EUGENE: "ROOTA TOOT - TOOT..." - Color Woodcut

COLEMAN, FLOYD W.: "IN THE PARK" - Color Linocut

COMPTON, LAWRENCE WM.: "UNTITLED" - Etching

DRISKELL, DAVID C.: "STILL LIFE WITH FRUIT" - Woodcut

DUNN, EUGENIA V.: "SHADOWS" - Linocut

EPTING, MARION A.: "TOTEM" - Lithograph

FERGUSON, CHARLES: "UNTITLED" - Etching

GLOVER, ROBERT: "CITY" - Linocut

HARREL, HUGH: "JANIE" - Sculp Metal Print

HARRIS, SCOTLAND: "JAZZ PLAYER" - Woodcut

HAWKINS, EUGENE: "TAKE NOTE" - Linocut

HENDERSON, LEROY W.: "LIFT US, WE PRAY" - Linocut

HICKS, LEON N.: "LITTLE BIRD" - Etching

HOLLINGSWORTH, ALVIN: "LONELY WOMAN" - Color Woodcut

HUNT, RICHARD: "UNTITLED" - Color Lithograph

JAMES, WILMER: "UNTITLED" - Serigraph

JOHNSON, MILTON: "LIMITED" - Woodcut

JORDAN, JACK: "GOING HOME" - Linocut

KINNEY, RICHARD: "SPRING" - Color Woodcut

MACKLIN, ANDERSON: "AT NOON TIME" - Etching

MC CULLOUGH, GERALDINE: "BLACK DIAMOND" - Color Woodcut

MC NEIL, WILLIAM: "LIBERA NOS A MALO" - Woodcut

MC NEILL, LLOYD: "LADY IN LABOR"- Relief Etching

MEO, YVONNE: "STRINGS" - Serigraph

MORGAN, NORMA: "DARK HEIGHTS" - Copper Engraving

MOSELY, JIMMIE: "CONTEMPLATION" - Woodcut

NELLS, JAMES L.: "BRIDGE FANTASY" - Wood Engraving

PERRY, MICHAEL K.: "TWO FIGURES" - Intaglio Print

PHILLIPS, HARPER T.: "FLIGHT" - Color Woodcut

POPE, ALVIN: "GIRL" - Serigraph

PUSEY, MAVIS: "UNTITLED" - Color Lithograph

PYBURN, DON: "MATHEW HENSON" - Linocut

RIDDLE, JOHN: "BILLY RENE" - Etching

ROGERS, CHARLES D.: "AN ADAPTION FROM THE THEME
OF THE PRODIGAL SON BY MURILLO" - Woodcut

SAAR, BETYE: "SAMSARA" - Color Etching

SATCHELL, ERNEST: "WORKING IN THE FIELD" - Woodcut

SIMON, JEWEL W,: "WALK TOGETHER CHILDREN" - Monoprint

SLATER, VAN: "EULA SEATED" - Woodcut

SMITH, FRANK E.: "CITY" - Linocut

SMITH, WILLIAM E.: "PAY-DAY" - Linocut

SMOCK, SUE JANE M.: "PRIESTESS OF OROSUN" - Woodcut

SNOWDEN, SYLVIA: "MOUNTAIN MAN" - Etching

SOARES, LAURA: "SUMMER" - Serigraph

STEPHENS, DAVID F.: "OLIVER G. PERRY" - Color Cardboard-
Relief Cut

WADDY, RUTH G.: "MATTER OF OPINION" - Color Linocut

WILLIAMS, WILLIAM: "UNTITLED" - Etching

WILSON, FRED: "THREE IN ONE" - Woodcut

WILSON, JOHN: "LA CALLE" - Color Lithograph

YATES, CHARLES E.: "SELF PORTRAIT" - Etching

YEARGANS, HARTWELL: "FOLKSINGER" - Color Linocut

The BOOK • The ARTISTS • AND The Techniques OF PRINT-MAKING

It is natural that "PRINTS BY AMERICAN NEGRO ARTISTS" should be born in California, in Los Angeles, a leading center, if not the leading center, of printmaking in the United States; the home of Sister Mary Corita of Immaculate Heart; the home of Tamarind, workshop for the master artists and the master printer. It is also natural that "PRINTS BY AMERICAN NEGRO ARTISTS" is a production of "CULTURAL EXCHANGE CENTER", which always put great emphasis on "Prints" in its Exhibits and its quarterly "CULTURAL ECHO".

And again it is natural that "Prints by American Negro Artists" is being edited by Dr. T.V.Roelof-Lanner. Dr. Roelof-Lanner published the first "AMERICAN BLOCK PRINT CALENDAR" in 1935, and in 1937 "AMERICAN BLOCK PRINTS". Dr. Roelof-Lanner did a "first" by publishing "PRINTS BY CALIFORNIA ARTISTS" in 1954. Many of the names of the contributing artists in that book have since become synonymous with printmaking. He brought a wealth of artistic and technical knowledge to "PRINTS BY AMERICAN NEGRO ARTISTS".

Prints are to the art world what chamber music is to the music world. Yet, despite the esoteric connotation, prints, one of the most creative art forms, are available to the public for their homes and private collections at modest prices. The value of the print increases with the artist's growth. The subject may range from representative to non-objective; from black and white to a riot of color; from small to mural size.

What is this creative art form, the print? Probably the oldest printed impression is the wood cut and the wood engraving. A wood cut is made from a wood block cut plankwise. The artist uses sharp knives, gouges, chisels, to cut away the surfaces that he does not want for his design. For wood engraving, the wood block is cut crosswise and the white lines made by a fine graving tool provides the design.

Engraving copper requires great skill. It is done with fine graving needles. The artist then inks the plate and the design is impressed on dampened paper in an etching press.

An etching is made by putting an acid-resistant coating on a copper or zinc plate. The artist cuts through the coating with an etching needle burin, graver or any sharp instrument. The plate is then immersed in an acid bath which eats away the copper or zinc. After washing and removing the coating, the artist inks the plate and the design is impressed on dampened paper in an etching press.

A dry point is made on metal plates, copper preferred. The artist uses a dry point needle, drawing directly on the plate. The dry point needle makes fine metal deposits on either side of the lines drawn by the artist; this deposit is called a "burr". When the plate is inked, the ink in the "burr" creates a soft, velvety line on the design which is impressed on dampened paper.

A lithograph is literally a stone drawing. The artist draws on a lithographic stone with a grease crayon. The stone is sponged with water rolled with a grease ink which rejects the wet, blank spaces. Dampened paper and a press complete the print.

Serigraph means writing on silk. On a tightly streched silk screen frame, the artist paints out all the parts of the design he does not want printed with a plastic or glue film. He then forces paint through the silk meshes with a squeegee to the paper placed below the screen.

There are variants of print mediums. Lino-cut (linoleum) and composition board, or scratch board are variants of wood cut or wood engraving. Intaglio is a variant of etching, and so on. There are interesting combinations of print media also, such as Eugene Hawkin's lino-cut on photo-litho.

As one can see from above, tremendous craftmanship as well as creativity is demanded of the printmaker. The Negro artist adds still another dimension, and the prints are all the more exciting for it, for, willingly or not, he is aware of the 20th Century technosociological struggle.

Brumsic Brandon's lino-cuts (cover), Mel Carey's scratch board ''Hunger'', Jewel Simon's collograph ''Walk Together Children'', Eugene Hawkin's lino-cut on photo-lithograph ''Take Note'', Don Pyborn's beautiful lino-cut ''Matthew Henson'' are a few of the prints illustrating this awareness.

This collection of prints by contemporary artists has tried to focus attention on the young artist. The names of the artists Charles White, Charles Alston, Robert Blackburn, Jacob Lawrence, John Biggers, Dox Thrash, Elton Fax have been recognized in the print world for many years. In fact there are other excellent artists who need to be brought to the public's attention.

The craftsman-like printing of Milton Johnson, Richard Kinney, Norma Morgan, Alvin C. Hollingsworth, Eugene Cheltenham, Eugene Hawkins, is unsurpassed by anyone, anywhere. Sylvester Britton, Brumsic Brandon, Calvin Burnett, Van Slater, Betye Saar, Richard Hunt, Emma Amos, Mavis Pusey, Joyce Cadoo and Floyd Coleman are also meticulous craftsmen which enhances their creativity.

Using other than the traditional printing media is a property of print making. Hugh Harrell uses sculp-metal for his prints; Floyd Coleman pulls prints from plaster blocks; Eugenia V. Dunn, Jewel Simon, Alvin C. Hollingsworth and Eugene Hawkins are also among the artists who experiment with new materials. Eugene Cheltenham does his color wood cuts on one block by cutting the main color, printing it, then cutting and printing the next color and so on. This is much more difficult than the usual way of cutting a separate block for each color. Lawrence Compton's untitled etching was done long before the non-objective concept in prints became popular.

In spite of their youth, all the artists in this collection are well known locally, and many are represented in permanent collections in our national museums. Some of them have international representation; among these are John T. Biggers, Calvin Burnett, David C. Driskell, Richard Hunt, Geraldine Mc Cullough, Norma Morgan, Jimmie Mosely, Michael K. Perry, Harper T. Phillips, Betye Saar, Sue Jane M. Smock, David Stephens, James L. Wells.

The range of prints in this book includes the sensitivity of a Charles E. Yates; the power of a Mavis Pusey, Jimmie Mosely; the superb copper engraving of a Norma Morgan; the color of a Laura Soares, Yvonne Meo, Calvin Burnett, Emma Amos; the black and white nuance of a Milton Johnson; the imagery of a Eugenia V. Dunn, James L. Wells.

This is a collection of the work of highly creative artists who were willing to undertake the difficulties of becoming skilled in the disciplines of their tools and media.

CULTURAL EXCHANGE CENTER can be proud to have filled a void by publishing "PRINTS BY AMERICAN NEGRO ARTISTS".

RUTH G. WADDY

CODTRIBUTIDG ARTISTS

RALPH ARNOLD

BORN: Chicago, Illinois, 1928

STUDIED: University of Illinois, The Hyde Park Art Center; The Art Institute of Chicago; B.A. Degree from Roosevelt University in 1955.

EXHIBITED: The Benjamin Gallery (All Collage Show 1965); 75th Anniversary Exhibit of the Chicago Society of Artists; The New Horizons in Sculpture, 1961 and 1964; Collage and Construction Show sponsored by the Hyde Park Art Center; Mundelein College, Chicago Craftsmen Exhibit: Rockford College Festival of the Arts, Rockford, Illinois; The Harper Gallery of Chicago; Exhibition Chicago 1965; Gallery-Mid North; One-Man Show Benjamin Galleries, Chicago; One-Man Show Greed Galleries, Rockford, Illinois, 1966.

AWARDS: Recipient of the Joseph Randall Shapiro Award in the 1965 Annual Exhibit of the Art Institute Alumni Association.

COLLECTIONS: Rockford College, Rockford, Illinois; The Contemporary Collection of American Works of the Museum of African Art, Washington, D.C.; many private collections.

POSITION: Ralph Arnold teaches collage techniques at the Country Side Gallery in Arlington Heights, Illinois; also has classes in his studio in Chicago; he has taught at the Hyde Park Art Center; member of the North Shore Art League; member of the Board of Directors of the Chicago Society of Artists; Associate Professor in Art, Rockford College, Rockford, Illinois.

PUBLICATIONS: Seven examples of Ralph Arnold's Collages and Constructions are included in the book "Collage and Found Art", which was published by Rheinhold and Company, 1964. He is also represented in "Prints by American Negro Artists", published by Cultural Exchange Center of Los Angeles, California.

JOHN T. BIGGERS

BORN: in Gastonia, North Carolina, 1924

STUDIED: Hampton Institute; Pennsylvania State University; University of Southern California.

EXHIBITED: 1966-New Faculty Show, University Wisconsin; 1966-Two-Man Show, Denver Art Museum; 1965-National & Regional Drawing Society Exhibition; 1965-Rockford College, Rockford, Illinois; 1963/64-USIs Traveling One-Man Show throughout Africa; 1963-One-Man Show, Lubbock Museum of Fine Arts; 1963-One-Man Show, Dallas Public Library; 1962-One-Man Show, Laguna Gloria Art Museum, Austin; 1962-One-Man Show,

Fort Woth Art Center; 1962-One-Man Show, Houston Museum of Fine Arts; 1960-AMSAC Exhibit, University of Pennsylvania, One-Man Show, Philadelphia Commercial Museum; 1952-"Texas Contemporary Artists" M.Kendler Co., New York, New York.

AWARDS: Unesco Fellowship-Artist's Study of Life in West Africa; Dallas Museum of Fine Arts Book Award: Best Designed Book, 1962; Theta Sigma Phi Writers Award: Best Book on Art in Texas, 1962; Piper Professor Award, 1962; The Architectural League's Honorable Mention in Mural Painting, 1955; Purchase Prizes: Houston Museum 1950, 1951, 1955; Dallas Museum, 1952; Atlanta University, 1950, 1953.

COLLECTIONS: Houston Museum; Dallas Museum; Lubbock Museum; Pennsylvania State University; Howard University; Atlanta University; Texas Southern University; Houston Public Library; Nina Cullinan; Susan McAshan; Max Lervine, Max Ernst; Mrs. Viktor Lowenfeld; Hampton Institute.

MURAL COMMISSIONS: Pennsylvania State University; Eliza Johnson Home for the Aged, Houston; YWCA, Houston; Carver High School, Naples, Texas; I.L.A. Local 872 Houston; Texas Southern University; Houston Public Library.

POSITION: Professor, Head Art Department, Texas Southern University since 1949; Houston Municipal Art Commissioner.

PUBLICATIONS: Books illustrated: The Good Earth, by Pearl Buck; New York: The Reader's Digest, 1966; I Momolu, by Lorenz Graham, New York, Crowell Co., 1966; Ananse, Web of Life in Africa.

CALVIN BURNETT

BORN: in Cambridge, Massachusetts, 1921

STUDIED: Boston University, M.F.A.; Boston Museum of Fine Arts School; Massachusetts School of Art; B.S. in Education.

MEMBER: Institute of Contemporary Art, Boston; Cambridge Art Association; Boston Printmakers (Bd. Dir.).

AWARDS: Atlanta University; Cambridge Centennial Exhibition; Cambridge Art Association; Germanic Museum (Cambridge); Wharton Settlement, Philadelphia; Busch-Reisinger Museum; Howard University; Association of American Artists.

EXHIBITED: Institute of Modern Art, Boston; Oakland Art Museum; National Academy of Design; Jordan Marsh Co.; Wellesley College; Atlanta University; Boston Public Library; American Federation of Arts traveling exhibition; Kiel Auditorium, St. Louis; San Francisco Art Association; Taller de Grafica, Mexico; Cambridge Art Association (one-man); Downtown Gallery, New York; Children's Art Center, Boston; Lewis School of Fine Arts (one-man); State Department traveling exhibition;

Institute of Contemporary Art, Boston; Library of Congress; Howard University; Boston University; Arthur Wood Gallery, Boston; and many others.

COLLECTIONS: Harvard University; Howard University; Wharton House, Philadelphia; Atlanta University; Lewis School, Boston; National Bezalel Museum, Jerusalem; Institute of Contemporary Art; Boston Printmakers Presentation Print; Boston Museum of Fine Arts; Fogg Museum of Art; Boston Public Library.

POSITION: Assistant Professor at the Massachusetts College of Arts since 1956.

BRUMSIC BRANDON JR.

BORN: in Washington, D.C.

STUDIED: New York University.

EXHIBITED: Times-Herald Outdoor Art Fair, Washington, D.C.; Corcoran Art Gallery, Washington, D.C.; CUNF Americana Hotel, New York City; Gallery Jae - St Albans, N.Y.

AWARDS: Varieties Key, N.Y.U.

POSITION: Designer Animator.

PUBLICATIONS: Saturday Review; Washington Post; Mademoiselle; Freedomways; Ebony; Magazine Digest; "Some of my best Friends", (Self Published 1963).

FLOYD W. COLEMAN

BORN: in Sawyerville, Alabama, 1939

STUDIED: A.B., Alabama State College; M.S., University of Wisconsin; Summer Study, Emory University, 1965 and 1966.

EXHIBITED: Atlanta University's Annual Exhibition of Negro Artists, 1956, '60, '61, '63, '64, '65. Young America Exhibition, New Orleans, La.; National Watercolor Show, Periora, Ill.; Landmarks of Milwaukee Exhibition, Milwaukee, Wis.; Mammouth Life Insurance Co. Exhibition, Milwaukee, Wis.; Four Arts Society Exhibition, Palm Beach, Fla.; 20th American Drawing Annual, Norfolk, Va.; One-man Show, Adairs Art Gallery, Artist's Teachers I Exhibition, High Museum, Atlanta, Ga.; Worlds Fair, New York; One-man Show, Florida AHM University, Tallahassee, Fla.; One-man Show, Elizabeth City State College, Elizabeth City, N.C.;Several One and Two-man Shows at Clark College since 1962; and many other exhibitions.

AWARDS: First Award in Watercolor, Atlanta University' National Exhibition of Negro Artists, 1964; John Hope Prize in Oils, Atlanta University' National Exhibition of Negro Artists, 1965.

COLLECTIONS: Public: Atlanta High Museum: Atlanta University collection; Private: Dr.Wiley S.Bolden; Dr.John Withers; Dr.C.Eric Lincoln; Dr.Melvin Drimmer; Dr.Esther Jackson; and many others.

POSITION: Assistant Professor and Acting Chairman, Department of Art, Clark College, Atlanta, Georgia.

LAWRENCE WM. COMPTON

BORN: in Beaumont, Texas, 1931

STUDIED: 3 years California School of Fine Arts.

EXHIBITED: One Man Show, Lucien Labaudt Art Gallery, San Francisco; One-Man Show, The 6 Gallery, San Francisco; USA Group Regional Show, Action Painters of Nothern California; Group Regional Show, 6 Gallery San Francisco; Rental Gallery Bay Artist, San Francisco Museum of Art; Group Show, Camino Gallery, New York; Group Show, Parma Gallery, New York; Group Show, The Market Place Gallery, New York; One-Man Show, The Market Place Gallery, New York; The American Negro Artist Looks At Africa, Commercial Museum, Philadelphia, Pennsylvania; Negroes On The American Scene, Americana Hotel, New York; One-Man Show, Family Savings, Los Angeles; California; Group Show, Prints of the Print Club Muenchen, Worms, Germany; Group Show, Prints "Leibl To To-Day", Bamberg and Ludwigshafen, Germany; Group Show, Oils, "Fall-Salon", House of Art, Muenchen, Germany; One-Man Show, Prints and Drawings, Cultural Exchange Center, Stuttgart, Germany; Group Show, Christmas-Show, Friends of Young Art, Lehnbach House, Muenchen, Germany.

AWARDS: Certificate of Excellence Exhibit for sculpture 1949; San Francisco Chronicle for sculpture 1949 Certificate of Merit; Scholastic Magazine 1949; Bank Prize for Painting San Francisco Art.

COLLECTIONS: Lehnbach Gallery; Friends of Young Art Club; New Munich Gallery; Engelhorn, Gallery Club; Handwerk, Insel Film; others.

REMARKS: Is collected by the City-Owned Lehnbach Gallery (which has the big Kandinsky Collection) as the first Negro-Artist and was shown also as the first Negro in The House of Art (Haus der Kunst).

PUBLICATIONS: in 2 Booklets: Compton's Motion-Art by G. Frankenberg.

DAVID C. DRISKELL

BORN: in Eatonton, Georgia, 1931

STUDIED: Skowhegan School of Painting and Sculpture (Colby College), Maine; A.B. in Fine Arts, Howard University, 1955; M.F.A., The Catholic University of America, Washington, D.C., 1962.

EXHIBITED: Atlanta University, Atlanta, Georgia; Barnett Aden Gallery, Washington, D.C.; Carver Museum (Tuskegee), Tuskegee, Alabama; Corcoran Art Gallery, Washington, D.C.; Dupont Theater Gallery, Washington D.C.; Fourier Gallery, College of Notre Dame, Baltimore, Maryland (One-man Show); Howard University Gallery of Art, Washington, D.C.; Lincoln University Gallery, Missouri; National Museum, Smithsonian Institution, Washington, D.C.; Portland Museum of Art, Maine; Colby College, Waterville, Maine; Savery Art Gallery, Talladega College, Talladega, Alabama; Rhodes National Gallery, Salisbury, Southern Rhodesia; King George VI Gallery, Port Elizabeth, South Africa; One-man Show, Carl Van Vechten Gallery of Art, Fisk University, 1964; One-man Show, Mt. St. Joseph College, Cincinnati, Ohio, 1964; Baltimore Museum, 1965; Franz Bader Gallery, 1965; Art in Embassies, USA, 1966; Oakland Art Museum, 1966; San Diego Fine Arts Gallery, 1966.

SCHOLARSHIPS: Scholastic Scholarship in Art, Howard University, 1952-55; Skowhegan School of Painting and Sculpture Scholarship, 1953; Special Study Grant, $3,500, Danforth Foundation to The Catholic University of America, 1961-62; Fellowship For Summer Study, Netherlands Institute of the History of Art, The Hague, 1964; Rockefeller Foundation Grant, $2,000 for European Museum Visitation, 1964.

AWARDS: Bocour Progress Award in Art, Skohegan, 1953; Charles W. Allen Award in Art, Howard University, 1954-1955; John Hope Award in Art, Atlanta University, 1959; 2nd Award in Graphic Arts, Atlanta University, 1961; Museum Donor Award, $200, American Federation of Arts, 1962; Museum Donor Purchase Award, $400, American Federation of Arts, 1964; Honorable Mention in Graphic Art, The Corcoran Gallery, 1965.

LECTURES: Tougaloo Southern Christian College, Tougaloo, Mississippi; Atlanta University, Atlanta, Georgia; Colorado College, Colorado Springs, Colorado; Mercer University, Macon, Georgia; Bennett College, Greensboro, North Carolina; Virginia Union University, Richmond, Virginia; Bowie State Teachers College, Bowie, Maryland.

COLLECTIONS: Work in Following Permanent Collections: Howard University Gallery of Art; Corcoran Art Gallery; Barnett Aden Gallery; Skowhegan School Collection; Savery Art Gallery; Danforth Foundation; Atlanta University Collection; Bocour Art Collection; LeMoyne College Collection; and private collections.

POSITIONS: Former Associate Professor and Head, Department of Art, Talladega College, Talladega, Alabama; Seven years of teaching experience in the History of Art and the Applied Arts of Painting, Graphics, Ceramics and Art Education; Three years Administrative work as Dean of Men at Talladega College and Director of the Talladega College Self-Study financed by a $25,000 Grant from the Danforth Foundation, 1959-61. First Lieutenant, U.S.A.R. and for two years teacher of Arts and Crafts (1954-55) with the D.C. Recreation Department, Washington, D.C.; Former Associate Professor and Acting Head, Department of Art, Howard University, Washington, D.C.; Presently Chairman, Department of Art, Fisk University, Nashville, Tennessee.

EUGENIA V. DUNN

BORN: in Henderson, Kentucky, 1916

STUDIED: Public School Systems of Henderson and Louisville; University of Louisville, B.S. (Louisville Municipal College); Art Instructions Inc., Certificate in Painting and Related Arts; Atlanta University, M.S.; further study at University of Michigan; student of Leo Katz, renown, artist of New York, New York (born in Austria).

EXHIBITED: Group Shows: Atlanta University; Tuskegee Institute; Veterans Administration Hospital, Tuskegee; Beaux-Arts Guild, Tuskegee; Kentuckianna Annual Exhibition, Louisville, Kentucky; State Fair, Louisville; Howard University, Washington, D.C.; Lincoln University, Jefferson City, Missouri; Cronon Gallery, Louisville; High Schools in Tuskegee; Bellarmine College, Louisville, Kentucky; Southern Indiana Studio, New Albany, Indiana; Atlanta's Piedmont Park; Louisville's Central Park; Downtown Bank, Little Rock; In groups or Two-Man, Four-Man Shows in Churches and Community Centers; Two-Man Show Spelman College; One-Man Shows: Downtown Clothing Store, Louisville; Adair's Downtown Gallery, Atlanta, Georgia; West Virginia State College; Philander Smith College in cooperation with Annual Arkansas State Festival of Arts; Texas Southern University, Morgan State College; Arkansas Arts Center, Little Rock.

AWARDS: Art major field of interest upon graduation from Junior High School - won First Prize in Art at the age of 13 in all city competition; Won the coveted President's Award for leadership, scholarship and citizenship (President of University of Louisville).

COLLECTIONS: Private and Public.

POSITION: Chairman of the Art Department Philander Smith College, Little Rock, Arkansas.

PUBLICATIONS: "American Negro Art" first printed in England; NCA Print Journal 1963; Portfolio Number One "The Atlanta Show", 1964; Cultural Exchange Center, Los Angeles, California "Prints by American Negro Artists".

REMARKS: Every person who is endowned with some talent, should work for universality in communication and human understanding in all disciplines, in order that men may make their contributions in their own way and enjoy a measure of happiness in this age of speed and dehumanization.

MARION A. EPTING

BORN: in Forest, Mississippi, 1940

STUDIED: Los Angeles City College; Otis Art Institute.

CHARLES FERGUSON

BORN: in New York City, 1927

STUDIED: High School Music and Art; Art Students League; School of Visual Arts; Cooper Union.

EXHIBITED: Group Shows.

POSITION: Teacher at the High School of Art and Design; Part of one of the Anti Poverty Programs teaching art on a High School level.

SCOTLAND HARRIS

BORN: in Baltimore, Maryland

STUDIED: Undergraduate study - Maryland State College, Princess Anne, Maryland; Graduate work - University of Maryland, College Park, Maryland.

EXHIBITED: Atlanta University, Atlanta, Georgia; Wicomico Art League, Salisbury, Maryland; University of Delaware, Newark, Delaware; Maryland State College, Princess Anne, Maryland; Cambridge Art League, Cambridge, Maryland; Laurel Kiwanis Club, Laurel, Delaware; Baltimore Outdoors Arts Festival, Baltimore, Maryland; Annual Arts Festival, Baltimore, Maryland.

AWARDS: Final competition, Atlanta University, "Jazz Player", Woodcut; Third place, Baltimore Annual Arts Festival, "Capitol Snow Scene", Honorable mention, Maryland State Awards Assembly, "Proximity", Collage; Honorable mention, Wicomico Art League, "Proximity", Collage; University of Delaware Regional Art Exhibition; "Chicago Fire", a collage, was selected by the jury for final exhibition.

COLLECTIONS: Wood sculptures, Prints, Paintings, Mosaic Composition, Modern pottery, Works done in various art media in private collections.

POSITION: Art Department Head, Margaret Brent High School (Helen, Maryland); Freelance Artist and Photographer.

EUGENE HAWKINS

BORN: in Los Angeles, California, 1933

STUDIED: Los Angeles City College; Los Angeles State College.

AWARDS: Freedom Foundation Award (political and editorial cartooning); first $3,000 award of John Hay Whitney Fellowship (1965).

EXHIBITED: Eight One-man shows (1957-1959); numerous group shows.

POSITION: Art Director, Jazz Festival, Hollywood Bowl.

LEROY W. HENDERSON

BORN: in Richmond, Virginia, 1936

STUDIED: B.S. Fine Arts Education, Virginia State College, Petersburg, Va., M.S. Fine Arts Education Pratt Institute, Brooklyn, N.Y.

POSITION: High School Art Teacher, New York City.

ALVIN HOLLINGSWORTH

BORN: in New York City, 1928

STUDIED: City College of New York, B.F.A., M.A. (Art Education); currently in doctoral program (Fine Arts), New York University.

AWARDS: Emily Lowe Award; John Hay Whitney Fellowship; Technicraft Award.

EXHIBITED: Jewish Museum; Brooklyn Museum; Museum of African Art, Washington, D.C.; Terry Dintenfass Gallery, New York; Gallery Herve, Paris; Ward Eggleston Gallery, New York; and other exhibitions.

COLLECTIONS: Brooklyn Museum; Museum of African Art, Washington, D.C.; General Electric Co.; and private collections.

POSITION: Instructor, High School of Art and Design, New York.

RICHARD HUNT

BORN: in Chicago, Illinois, 1935

STUDIED: Art Institute of Chicago, B.A.E.

AWARDS: James Nelson Raymond Foreign Traveling Fellowship; Guggenheim Fellowship; Tamarind Fellowship.

EXHIBITED: Alan Gallery, New York (one-man); B.C.Holland Gallery, Chicago (one-man); University of Tulsa (one-man); The Museum of Modern Art; International Exhibition of Painting and Sculpture, Carnegie Institute; Whitney Museum of American Art; Solomon R.Guggenheim Museum; Seattle World's Fair; Art Institute of Chicago; Felix Landau Gallery, Los Angeles.

COLLECTIONS: The Museum of Modern Art and permanent collections of many art museums in United States and Europe.

MILTON JOHNSON

BORN: in Milwaukee, Wisconsin, 1932

STUDIED: Wisconsin; Boston; Tokyo, Japan.

EXHIBITED: In U.S. and Japan.

AWARDS: Numerous in Graphic Arts, Painting, Drawing since 1950.

COLLECTIONS: Private: U.S. and Japan.

POSITION: Boston Museum School and Boston Museum Design
Department.

JACK JORDAN

BORN: in Wichita Falls, Texas.

STUDIED: A.B. in Art, Langston University; M.A. in Art Education,
Iowa University; M.F.A. in Sculpture: Thesis "An Approach to Sculpture",
Stato University of Iowa; Has done further study in Sculpture and Graphics
at Oklahama University.

EXHIBITED: Jordan's creations have been exhibited in 22 states: 18
One-Man exhibitions; numerous cash commissions; 14 invitational exhibitions; and 14 art museums of which he has received over 30 Art awards
of local, regional, national, and intergrated competition. Along with leading American Artists, Jack Jordan exhibited in New York City, Architectural league, National Sculpture Society; Internationale Buchkunst Aus-
stellung, Leipzig, Germany; Jonylyn Art Museum, Omaha, Nebraska; Providence Rhode Island Gallery; Philadelphia, Pennsylvania Commercial
Art Museum; Nelson Art Gallery, Kansas City, Missouri; State University
of Iowa Art Gallery, Iowa City, Iowa; Atlanta University Art Gallery,
Atlanta, Georgia; Philbrook Art Museum, Tulsa, Oklahoma; Reno Russo
Studio, Clarksville, Tennessee; Gibbes Art Gallery, Charleston, South
Carolina; Louisiana State University Invitational Art Exhibition, Baton
Rouge, Louisiana; Oklahoma Art Center, Oklahoma City, Oklahoma; In-
formation and Education Center, Ft. Campbell, Kentucky; Walker Art
Center, Minneapolis, Minnesota; Texas Southern University Art Gallery,
Houston, Texas; New Vistas of American Art, Howard University, Wash-
ington, D.C.; Emancipation Contennial National Art Exhibition, Chicago,
Illinois; Wayne College Art Gallery, Detroit, Michigan; Beaux Arts Guild,
Tuskegee, Alabama; Philander Smith College Art Gallery, Little Rock,
Arkansas; Lincoln University Art Gallery, Jefferson City, Missouri; Vir-
ginia Highlands Art Festival, Abington, Virginia; El Mira Art Gallery,
Pismo Beach, California. Presently three of his prints are on display in
Russia. It will travel with exhibits in Lenningrad, Baker, Alma-Ata,
Prague, and Moscow.

AWARDS: In addition to the extended list (from 1949-1965) of achievements and honors, Jack Jordan has also been successful in 1966: He has
added four prizes to his awards list, two of which were awarded at the
El mira Art Gallery in Atlanta University. Last year he won the top cash
prize in the latter exhibition. Adding to his list of commissions, he recently received a substantial sculpture commission which has financed
his trip to Africa to attend the First World's Festival of Negro Art. Jack
Jordan was also one of eight recently honored for outstanding achievements and destinction in respective fields by Sigma Lambda Chapter of
Alpha Phi Alpha Fraternity, Inc.

POSITION: Jack Jordan is a member of Alpha Phi Alpha Fraternity, Inc., the Masonic Lodge, and he is the National Chairman of the Conference of Artists, chairman of the Commission on Missions for Bothany Church, and co-chairman of the committee for the development of Art in Negro Colleges.

PUBLICATIONS: Jack Jordan is listed in Who's Who in American Education, Inc. Volume XVIII; A print protfolio by Negro Artists; National Conference of Artists, Margaret Burrough - Editor; "Great Negroes Past and Present", Russell Adams; "Prints by American Negro Artists", T.V. Roelof - Lanner Ph.D. - Editor, published by the Cultural Exchange Center of Los Angeles, California (Rosemarie von Studnitz, President); Delta Phi Delta National Honorary Art Fraternity; and minor listings.

RICHARD KINNEY

BORN: in Detroit, Michigan, 1933

STUDIED: B.F.A. Wayne State University, 1954; M.A. Wayne State University, 1955.

EXHIBITED: 1952 - Oil painting - Terry National Exhibition, Miami, Honorable Mention - Juried; 1953 - Woodcut - 44th Annual Michigan Artists Exhibit, Detroit - Juried; 1954 - Watercolor - 11th Annual Scarab Club Watercolor Exhibition, Detroit - Juried; 1954 - Woodcut - 45th Annual Michigan Artists Exhibition, Detroit - Juried; 1955 - 6 works (various media). Annual "Young Detroiters Exhibition", Detroit Artists Market - Juried; 1955 - Woodcut - 1st Graphics Exhibition, Texas Western College - Juried; 1955 - One - Man Exhibition, Asbury College, Kentucky; 1955 - Woodcut - 46th Annual Michigan Artists Exhibit, Detroit - Juried; 1956 - Woodcut - 1st National Print Exhibition, Silvermine Guild of Artists, Connecticut - Juried; 1956 - One - Man Exhibition, Jam Handy Gallery; 1956 - Woodcut - 40th Annual Exhibition of the Society of American Graphic Artists, New York - Juried; 1957 - Woodcut - 48th Annual Michigan Artists Exhibition, Detroit - Juried; 1957-1958 - Various works exhibited with Arts Extended Group, Detroit; 1958-1965 - Various works exhibited with Wayne State University Faculty, Detroit; 1960 - Oils - exhibited with Wayne State University Faculty, Central Michigan University, Pleasant Ridge, Michigan; 1961 - Oil painting - 51st Annual Michigan Artists Exhibition, Detroit - Juried; 1961 - Oil painting - West Michigan Art Exhibition, Grand Rapids - Juried; 1962 - 40 works - One - Man Exhibit at AAA Gallery, Detroit; 1963 - Woodcut - Hanover College Graphic Arts Exhibit, Hanover, Indiana.

COLLECTIONS: Many private collections all over USA.

POSITION: Art Director, Wayne State University Press; Instructor, Department of Art and Art History, Wayne State University.

ANDERSON MACKLIN

BORN: in Luther, Oklahoma, 1933

STUDIED: Lincoln University of Missouri, B.S.; University of Missouri M.A.; The Pennsylvania State University.

EXHIBITED: Dallas Museum of Fine Arts; Atlanta Annual; University of Missouri; Lincoln University; Wiley College; Mississippi Valley State College; The Pennsylvania State University; Missouri State Fair; Cole County Fair of Missouri; Petersburg Annual; Friends of Petersburg Show; Virginia State College; Virginia Union University; Glendale Museum.

AWARDS: First prize, Oil, Cole County Fair of Missouri; First prize, Water-Color, County Fair of Missouri; Second prize, Water-Color, Missouri State Fair; Second prize, Ceramics, Petersburg Annual.

COLLECTIONS: Lincoln University of Missouri; Dr. G.W. Johnson, Maryland State University; Mr. J. Brandon, Ettrick, Virginia; and other private collections.

POSITION: Instructor of Art Education, Virginia State College, Petersburg, Virginia.

WILLIAM McNEIL

BORN; in Austin, Texas, 1935

STUDIED: Valley College - A.A. Degree - 1959; Chouinard Art Institute - B.F.A. Degree - 1963; U.S.C. - Teaching Credential - 1966.

EXHIBITED: Los Angeles Art Association (Print Show); Brand Library, Glendale, California (One-Man Show); Frye Art Museum, Seattle, Washington (11th Annual); Gardena High School, Gardena, California (One-Man Show); West Coast Painters Exibition.

COLLECTIONS: Mrs. Alma Lansberger, Los Angeles, California; Dr. Estelle Hughes, Compton, California; Mr. & Mrs. Albert Waters, San Francisco, California; Miss Gwendelyn Keel, Los Angeles, California; etc.

REMARKS: People are my main concern; their environment, the seasons of the year and the sufferings of the heart.

LLOYD McNEILL

BORN; in Washington, D.C., 1935

STUDIED: Morehouse College, B.A.; Howard University, M.F.A.; Ecole des Beaux Arts, Paris.

AWARDS: First prize, Watercolor, Annual Southwest Art Exhibit, Washington, D.C.; Second prize, Oil, First Annual Buchanan Art Exhibit, Rockville, Maryland; Grant-in-aid, Atlanta Arts Festival.

EXHIBITED: Barnett-Aden Gallery; Atlanta Festival; La Grange College; Atlanta University (one-man); Howard University (one-man); Dartmouth College (one-man); Green Mountain Junior College (one-man); Spelman College (one-man); UCLA Galleries.

COLLECTIONS: William B.Jaffe, New York; Spelman College; Dartmouth College; Atlanta Art Museum; King and Queen of Sikkim; Le Havre Museum, France.

YVONNE MEO

BORN: in Seattle, Washington, 1929

STUDIED: UCLA; USC, California State College at Los Angeles, California; Polytecnic Nationale in Mexico City; Otis Art Institute in Los Angeles, California; M.A. degree in Fine Arts.

EXHIBITED: All Juried Shows: Ankrum Gallery; Le Dilettante (one woman show) 1965; Westwood Art Association Gallery (one woman show) 1966; Los Angeles Art Association Gallery 1965; The Graphic International Exhibit in Leipzig, Germany 1965; UCLA print show 1966; The Tower Gallery in Los Angeles City Hall 1966; Redondo Beach Art Festival 1966; United Design Associates show rooms (one woman show) 1966; Bullocks, Sloanes, Pasadena Art Festival 1966; Hollywood Bowl 1966; Recent Exhibit: 3 paintings in The Negro in American Art Exhibition which started September 12th at Dickson Gallery at UCLA sponsored by Dr. Frederick S. Wight. The exhibit travels to Berkeley, University of California at Davis, Fine Arts Gallery of San Diego, and Oakland Art Museum.

AWARDS: Scholarship to Otis Art Institute at age of 13 years; Regional and National Scholarship from Delta Signa Theta, Sorority while attending UCLA - Art Major; Judges Award 1966 at Hollywood Bowl Art Festival 1966; Special Award 1966 at Hollywood Bowl Art Festival 1966; Second place cash award by California Fine Arts Gallery at the Pasadena Art Festival 1966; Honorable Mentions in Westwood Art Association's Print and Graphic Exhibit 1966; Cited by the Los Angeles Authors Study Club for outstanding contributions and achievements in the field of art 1966; Honored by the Delta Sorority and cited by Mayor Sam Yorty at City Hall for painting "Urban Renewal" which was juried for the Tower Gallery February 1966; Invited to show graphics in the graphic exhibition in Moscow, Russia, 1966.

COLLECTIONS: California Fine Arts Gallery in Pasadena; United Design Associates Show Room in Beverly Hills; Mr. Roy Wilkins, executive director of the National NAACP; Dr. Earl L. Woods, Psychiatrist of Bevly Hills; and many others.

POSITION: Instructor of Design Craft and Stage Design at Van Nuys Senior High School.

NEWS ITEMS and PUBLICATIONS: Motive Magazine; A Print Portfolio by Negro Artists by the National Conference of Artists; Art Forum; The

International Graphic Book Arts Catalogue, Leipzig, Germany; Hollywood Bowl Artist Series; Herald Examiner; Los Angeles Times; Pasadena Star Independent; Channel 2, Paul Udall, Big News; Yvonne Cole Meo was interviewed re UCLA Art Exhibit September to October 1966.

NORMA MORGAN

BORN: in New Haven, Connecticut, 1928

STUDIED: Art Students League of New York; Whitney School of Art; Hans Hoffman School of Fine Arts; Stanley Hayter's Atelier 17.

AWARDS: John Hay Whitney Fellowship; Tiffany Foundation Fellowship; Stacey Foundation Fellowship; Academic Artists Prize at Springfield Museum, Massachusetts; David Rose Award, New York; Gold Medal and First prize at American Artists Professional League, New York; Gold Medals at Audubon Show, New York.

EXHIBITED: Whitney Museum, New York; Associated American Artists Galleries, New York; Royal Society of Watercolour Painters, London; U.S. State Department's traveling show, Soviet Union; Institute of Graphic Arts, New York; New York World's Fair; UCLA Galleries.

COLLECTIONS: Brooklyn Museum; The Museum of Modern Art; Smithsonian Institution; International Graphic Art Society; National Gallery of Art, Washington, D.C.; Library of Congress; Boston Museum of Fine Arts; Philadelphia Museum; Walker Art Center; Howard University; Victoria and Albert Museum, London; and many other permanent collections in the U.S. and abroad.

JIMMIE MOSELY

BORN: in Lakeland, Florida, 1927

STUDIED: Texas Southern University, Houston, Texas; Pennsylvania State University, University Park, Pennsylvania; Rutgers University New Brunswick, New Jersey.

EXHIBITED: Atlanta University, Atlanta, Georgia; Centennial Exhibition Nelson Gallery and Atkins Museum, Kansas City, Missouri; University of Maryland, College Park, Maryland; University of Delaware, Newark, Delaware.

AWARDS: 3rd Prize in Prints, Atlanta University, 1954; 1st Prize in Watercolors, Atlanta University, 1963; 1st Prize in Watercolors, Atlanta University, 1965; 1st Prize in Watercolors and 1st Prize in Graphics, Emancipation Centennial National Exhibit, New Orleans, Louisiana.

POSITION: Assistant Professor and Director of Art Education at Maryland State College; President of the National Conference of Artist.

Mosely Elected to Head Art Association

Mr. Jimmie Mosely, head of the Art Education Department at Maryland State College, recently attended the National Conference of Artists Ninth Annual Meeting at Indiana University and came away in possession of the presidency of the organization.

The well known and much exhibited Eastern Shore artist will hold office for two years in this organization of artists which was founded in 1959 for the stimulation and promulgation of art created by Negroes. Originally intended to group those artists who had participated in the National Annual Exhibition for Negro Artists at Atlanta University, this organization now embraces all who have a sincere interest in the growth and development of young artists.

Mr. Mosely reports that the Fine Arts Department at Indiana University has received federal funds to improve creative work in Negro colleges. Dr. Mary Rouse, of that department, is currently at work on a study of Negro art programs and Dr. Henry Hope and Dr. Albert Elsen, chairman of the Fine Arts and the Art History departments, are readying a similar study. The motive for these programs is that the creative work in art at predominantly Negro colleges is a vital force in the integration process along with the objective of improving the position of the Negro artist in American life.

Mr. Mosely is one of the foremost spokesman of the developing quest for excellence among Negro artists and has led many of his students into the mainstream of American art today.

R. E. Smith
Director of Public Relations

JAMES L. NELLS

BORN: in Atlanta, Georgia, 1902

STUDIED: Lincoln University, Pa.; B.S. and M.A. from Columbia University, New York; with S.W. Hayter, "Atelier 17", N.Y. and the National Academy of Design, N.Y.

EXHIBITED: Soc. Washington Printmakers, 1962, 1963, 1964, Washington, D.C.; Washington Water Color Society; Smithsonian Institute; S.A.G.A. 1963, 1966; Har Zion Temple, Philadelphia, Pennsylvania, 1964, 1965; The 15th Area Exhibition, Corcoran Gallery of Art; Howard University Gallery of Art, 1962, 1965, 1966; Festival of Contemporary Religious Art, St. George's Episcopal Church, Fredericksburg, Virginia; African Traveling Exhibition of Paintings and Prints by International Art Groups and many others. One-Man Shows: Delphic Gallery of Art, New York, N.Y; Brooklyn Museum Summer Show; The Barnett Aden Gallery of Art, Washington, D.C.; The Smithsonian Institute (Graphic Arts Division), Washington, D.C.; The Howard University Gallery of Art; Spellman College, Atlanta University; Two-Man Show: The Art Gallery, Fisk University, Nashville, Tennessee.

AWARDS: Harmon Gold Medal for Distinguished Achievement among Negroes, Harmon Foundation, New York City; First Prize for work in black and white, Harmon Exhibition, New York City; Honorable Mention The Sixth Annual Area Exhibition, The Corcoran Gallery of Art, Washington, D.C; Second Prize for Religious Painting, Exhibition of Religious Painting, Federation of Churches; George F. Muth Prize for Engraving-Aquatint, Washington Water Color Club, Smithsonian Institute, Washington, D.C.; George F. Muth Purchase Prize, Washington, D.C.; First Merit Prize, Graphic Arts Category, Washington Area Religious Art Exhibition, Smithsonian Institute, Washington, D.C.; 2nd Prize for Graphic Works, Festival of Contemporary Religious Art, Fredericksburg, Virginia.

COLLECTIONS: Valentine Museum, Richmond, Virginia; Thayer Museum, University of Kansas; Hampton Institute, Virginia; Phillips Memorial Gallery, Washington, D.C.; Barnett Aden Art Gallery, Washington, D.C.; International Business Machine, New York City; Graphic Division, Smithsonian Institute, Washington, D.C.; Talladega College Gallery of Art and Fisk University Gallery of Art.

POSITION: Professor of Art, Howard University, Washington, D.C.

REMARKS: Form and its essence are the tools with which the artist works. The materials he uses should be subordinate to these. However, he should become their master and identify himself with them to the extent that they become a part of him.
With this merger the artist is at his best.
I feel that the plea for the artist is to be valued by his use of imagination and to create another nature out of the cultural material that nature gives. My concern has been with religious themes and with the drama of everyday life with special emphasis on Negro subjects.

MICHAEL K. PERRY

BORN: in Los Angeles, California, 1940

STUDIED: Los Angeles City College; Los Angeles State College, B.A. Otis Art Institute.

EXHIBITED: Tower Gallery - Negro History Week.

REMARKS: My prints are on display at the Julie Dohan Gallery, Sherman Oaks, California.

HARPER T. PHILLIPS

BORN: in Courtland, Alabama, 1928

STUDIED: Alabama State College, Montgomery, Alabama, B.S. 1951; New York University, M.A. 1957.

EXHIBITED: New Vistas in American Art, Howard University; Norfolk Museum, Norfolk, Virginia; Louisiana State Art Commission; Madison Gallery, New York; The Audubon Artists, National Academy Galleries; Atlanta University, Southeastern Art Association; Greater Gulf States Fair; Art Directions Gallery; Emancipation Centennial, Chicago, Illinois; Wiley College; Hampton Institute, Philander Smith; Artist Gallery, (Georgetown) Washington, D.C.; Artist Gallery, Virginia Beach, Virginia; Virginia Museum, Richmond, Virginia; Jackson State College; Lincoln University, Jefferson City, Missouri; American Federation of Artists; Fort Valley State College.

AWARDS: Atlanta University Annuals 1954, 1956, 1958, 1960; Mobile Art Festival; Greater Gulf States Fair; Art Directions Gallery; Springfield Art League; Emancipation Centennial; Deep South Artists and Writers Conference; The National Conference of Artists; The Contemporary Americans.

COLLECTIONS: Atlanta University; Hampton Institute; Artist Gallery; Art Directions Gallery; Alabama State College; Howard University; Jackson State College.

POSITION: Teacher, Board of Education, New York City; Art Curriculum Coordinator; Horace Mann - Lincoln Institute; Teachers College; Columbia University; Art Consultant for Childrens Community Art Exhibitions for Youth House and First National City Bank, New York City; Art Exhibition and Program Coordinator for Massive Economic Neighborhood Development Inc., New York City.

REMARKS: The Negro artist must weave together the double strand of minority and majority group experience and paint them in their mutually conditioning interaction. The story of the Negro artist must be seen in terms of a larger landscape of the growth and maturing of America. In this respect, the Negro artist must deal with the shadows and substances that affect Negro life in terms of an over - all perspective. This is the "Pilgrim Progress" of the modern Negro artist: to give universality to the particularity of his experience. The Negro artist must come to grips with the contradictions affecting Negro life. These contradictions must serve as potent - forces in his becoming a universal artist.

In terms of a creative synthesis, some horizons of Negro artists would be:
1) He must work and polish his technique, so that he may become the universal artist. His truth must be seen within a total framework. The Negro artist must seek for the drudging vision to pilfer from the universe meanings that are duralistic rather than individualistic.
2) The Negro artist must allow his work to be motivated by a thematic intuition. In this regard his paintings should swell from the deepest emotional reaches of personality. In this way, the artist will be able to search out, give rational meaning, and concretize the hopes, fears, joys of human existence.
3) The Negro must seek to allow his art to aid the growth of humanity. His progress must be toward a realistic idealism. This latter would mean the engagement of the intellect, the passion, the will, and the imagination

in the interpreting the real to the point that it takes on the spirit, stance, and overtones of the universal.

ALVIN POPE

BORN: in Baltimore, Maryland

STUDIED: Maryland State College, Princess Anne, Maryland.

EXHIBITED: Atlanta University; Maryland State College; University of Maryland, College Park, Maryland; University of Delaware, Newark.

AWARDS: First Prize Prints: Salisbury Art League Exhibit, Salisbury, Maryland.

MAVIS PUSEY

BORN: in Jamaica, West Indies, 1931

STUDIED: Art Students League, New York.

EXHIBITED: Art Students League, New York; Treasure Gallery, New Jersey; and other group shows.

COLLECTIONS: Will Barnet; Mr. Henry Sternberg, New York; Mrs. Rosina Lucash, New Jersey; Mrs. D.S.Cohen, California; Mr. E.H.Fletcher, Buenos Aires, Argentina; Mrs. Jack Dryfus, New York; Mr. Ed Aimone, Reno, Nevada.

CHARLES D. ROGERS

BORN: in Cherokee, Oklahoma, 1935

STUDIED: Private study, Hayel Shively, 1960 - 1961; B.A. California State College, Los Angeles, 1961 - 1963.

EXHIBITED: Oakland Fireman's Hall; Dooto's Music Center; De Voes Travel Agency; Security First National Bank, Rosecrans Branch; All City Art Festival, City Art Department.

AWARDS: Honorable mention, All City Art Show, 1965.

POSITION: Artist - Designer, Traid Corporation, Glendale, California

BETYE SAAR

BORN: in Los Angeles, California, 1929

STUDIED: Pasadena City College; UCLA, B.A.; now attending Long Beach State College for M.A.

AWARDS: First Prize - Graphics (1965) and Honorable Mention (1966), Miracle Mile of Art, Hollywood, California; First Prize, Los Angeles Area Print Exhibit; Purchase Prize, Los Angeles Outdoor Art Exhibit; Cash Award, Contemporary II Art Competition, Los Angeles.

EXHIBITED: Kozlow Gallery (one-man); Long Beach State College Drawing Exhibit; Miracle Mile of Art Exhibit; 2nd Annual All-California Print Exhibit; Contemporary I and II Art Exhibits; Los Angeles Outdoor Art Exhibit; Art on Paper, North Carolina; 5th Annual Mercyhurst National Exhibit, Pennsylvania; 20th National Exhibition of Prints, Washington, D. C.; National Black and White Print Exhibit, Kansas; and others.

PUBLICATIONS: Prints by American Negro Artists; Prize-Winning Graphics 1965.

JEWEL W. SIMON

BORN: in Houston, Texas, 1911

STUDIED: Atlanta University; Art Instruction, Inc., with Alice Bunbar; and Art Institute of Atlanta.

EXHIBITED: Atlanta University; Brand Library of Art and Music, Glendale, California; Associated Students Lounge, UCLA; Los Feliz Jewish Community Center.

VAN SLATER

BORN: in Los Angeles, California, 1941

STUDIED: University of California at Los Angeles, M.F.A.

MEMBER: Los Angeles County Art Association.

EXHIBITED: Brand Library of Art and Music, Glendale, California; Los Feliz Jewish Community Center.

WILLIAM E. SMITH

BORN: in Chattanoogo, Tennessee, 1913

STUDIED: Cleveland School of Art, Cleveland, Ohio; John Huntington Polytechnical Art Institute; Harold Cooper's School Advertising Art, Cleveland, Ohio; Chinuard Art Institute.

EXHIBITED: Cleveland Museum of Art; Dayton Art Institute Association American Artist, New York; National Academy of Design, New York;

Oakland Art Gallery; Library of Congress; Pennsylvania Academy of Art; Denver Museum; Atlanta University; Glendale Library; Tower Gallery Los Angeles City Hall; Connecticut Academy of fine Arts.

AWARDS: Three Certificates of Merit from Cleveland Museum of Art.

COLLECTIONS: Seven Prints Cleveland Museum of Art; One Print Library of Congress; One Print Howard University, Washington D.C.

POSITION: Graphic Lay-out Artist, Lockheed California Company, Burbank; President of Art-West Associated Inc.; Co-ordinated Arts & Crafts Exhibits for National Negro History Week 1964, 1965, 1966 - 1967 Los Angeles, California.

SUE JANE M. SMOCK

BORN: in New Orleans, Louisiana, 1937

STUDIED: Oberlin College, Oberlin, Ohio - B.A. 1958; Columbia University, New York, New York - M.A. 1959; School of Oriental and African Studies - 1961 of London University, London, England.

EXHIBITED: Oberlin College and Columbia U. galleries; The Cultural Institute, San Juan, Puerto Rico (during the Pablo Casals Festival); The Everson Museum of Art, Syracuse, New York; The Everhart Museum of Art, Scranton, Pennsylvania; The Museum of Art, the Munson-Williams-Proctor Institute, Utica, New York; The 33rd Gallery, New Orleans, Louisiana; One-Woman: Dillard University, New Orleans, Louisiana; Cornell University (Cornell United Religious Work) Ithaca, New York; Contemporary Trends, Ithaca, New York; The Woodstock Gallery, London, England; The Hotel Presidential Gallery, Enugu, Nigeria; The Smithsonian Institution, Washington, D.C.

COLLECTIONS: Oberlin College, Oberlin, Ohio; The Smithsonian Institution, Washington, D.C.; The Barnet-Aden Gallery, Washington, D.C.; Cornell University (Cornell United Religious Work) Ithaca, New York; Dartmouth College, Hanover, New Hampshire; Private collections.

REMARKS: I have spent much of my time, during the last five years, out of the United States. I have just returned from almost three years in West Africa; six months in England; three months in France; one month in Poland; three months in Switzerland, and the remainder in Italy and Spain. These years abroad have had direct bearing on my work, and my prints show a profound influence.

DAVID F. STEPHENS

BORN: in Washington, D.C., 1941

STUDIED: Howard University 1961-1965; Temple University 1959-1961.

EXHIBITED: Smithsonian Institute, University of Oklahoma; 8 National Printmakers Exhibition Oklahoma City; 1965 & 1966 4th Army Art Exhibition; 8 Young Printmakers Fisk University, Nashville, Tennessee.

AWARDS: 1st Place Annual Neighbors Show D.C. (Prints); 1st place 4th Army Exhibition 1966 (Prints).

COLLECTIONS: Various private.

REMARKS: Finishing tour in the Army and returning to school.

RUTH G. WADDY

BORN: in Lincoln, Nebraska, 1909

STUDIED: Famous Artists Home Study Course; Los Angeles City College; Otis Art Institute.

EXHIBITED: Graphik aus fuenf Kontinenten, Leipzig, Germany; Brand Library of Art and Music, Glendale, California; Associated Students Lounge, UCLA; Los Feliz Jewish Community Center, UCLA Galleries.

POSITIONS: Founder of Art-West Associated; collected prints for "Prints by American Negro Artists".

FRED WILSON

BORN: in Chicago, Illinois, 1932

STUDIED: Mt. San Antonio Jr. College; B.A. La Verne College; Two years graduate work at Fresno State College; Two years graduate work at Los Angeles State College.

EXHIBITED: 1960 - One-Man Show, California Hotel, Fresno, California; 1961 - One-Man Show, Griswold Stone Cellar, Claremont, California; One-Man Show, Ontario County Library, Ontario, California; 1962 - Los Angeles County Museum Design West Show; Afro-American Show, Shrine Auditorium, Los Angeles, California; 1963 - New York Museum /three months/ Los Angeles ALL CITY SHOW, Barnsdale, Los Angeles, California; One-Man Show, La Verne College, La Verne, California; 1964 - Los Angeles Negro History Week, City Hall, Los Angeles, California; One-Man Show, Family Savings & Loans, Los Angeles, California; 1965 - Ankrum Gallery, Los Angeles, California; Five-Man Show, Newhall, California; 1966 - Tower Gallery, City Hall, Los Angeles, California; Watts Rennaissance of the Arts, Los Angeles, California; Galleries of U.C.L.A; All City Show, Barnsdale, Los Angeles, California; Russia-American-Cultural-Exchange, Moscow, Russia.

AWARDS: Certificate of Merit, Latham Foundation; 31 First Prizes in Sculpture and Paintings; of all the major Fairs of California, Certificate of Merit in Sculpture; Los Angeles - Design West Show; Honorable mention for stone sculpture "Moon Man", Eagle Rock, California; Plaque SILVER BUNYOL, president of Valencia, Spain, contribution to the International Arts.

COLLECTIONS: "The Priest", Stone, Mrs. Marian Matthew, Los Angeles, California; "The Depth of Hell", Batik Print, Att. Sam Thompson, Newhall, California; "The Birds", Painting, Mrs. Terry Young, Newhall, California; "Sun Rise", Batik Print, Architect Hal Williams, Los Angeles, California; "Vanity Stairway", Woodblock Print, President Valencia, Spain.

POSITION: Professional with my own Accelerated Art Program, Newhall. California; Instructor at Wm. S. Hart High School, Newhall, California.

REMARKS: Statement of experience in Art: The ability to fluctuate from the Textile and Ceramic media back to Sculpture gives me flexibility in designs. Although, I am limited in materials -- both size and shape -- this renders me an opportunity to get the most out of a work. On occasions, I try to heighten the message of my sculpture by deforming the figures. My greatest inspiration for Sculpture is derived from people.

JOHN WILSON

BORN: in Boston, Massachusetts, 1922

STUDIED: School of the Museum of Fine Arts, 1944; Tufts University, B.S. in Education, 1947; Fernand Leger's School, Paris, France, 1949; Instituto Politecnico, Mexico City, 1952; Esmeralda School of Art, Mexico City, 1952; Escuela de las Artes del Libro, Mexico City, 1954 - 1955.

EXHIBITED: Atlanta University; Smith College; Wellesley College; Carnegie Institute Annual, 1944, 1945, 1946; The Negro Artist Comes of Age, traveling exhibit; Library of Congress National Print Exhibit, 1945, 1946; Institute of Modern Art, Boston, 1943, 1944, 1945; Group Exhibits at Boris Mirski Art Gallery, Boston, 1944, 1945, 1946, One-Man Show, 1946; Addison Gallery of American Art; Pepsi-Cola Annual; Museum of Modern Art, New York Master Prints from the Museum Collection; Metropolitan Museum of Art, New York Young American Painters; Society of American Etchers, Gravers, Lithographers and Woodcutters, Inc., New York, 1952, 1953, 1955; Traveling Exhibit of Contemporary American Prints, Paris, France, Bibliotheque National, 1951; Muses des Beaux-Arts Rouen, 1952; Dijon, 1953; Lyons, 1954; Library of Congress International Print Exhibit; Cincinnati Museum International Biennial of color lithography; Boston Printmakers Annual 1; Museum of Modern Art, New York "Young American Printmakers"; Art Wood Gallery, Boston, (One-Man Show); Exchange Exhibit of American Prints, Italy; National Academy of Design Special Exhibit of Prints; Brooklyn and Long Island Artists, Brooklyn Museum; 10th Annual South Shore Art Festival; Boston Printmakers Annual; National Academy of Design Annual, 1966.

AWARDS: Atlanta University's John Hope Award at 1st. National Art Exhibit; 2nd. National Exhibit, 1st. prize, Painting, 3rd. prize, Prints; 3rd. National Exhibit, 1st prize for the Best Portrait or Figure Painting; National Exhibit 1951 - 3rd prize, Prints; 1952 - 1st prize, Prints; 1954 - 1st prize, Prints; 1st prize, Watercolor; 1955 - 1st prize for the Best Portrait or Figure Painting; 1957 - 2nd prize, Watercolor; 1st prize, Prints; 1965 - 1st prize, Prints; 1966 - 2nd prize, Prints.
The James William Paige Traveling Fellowship for study in Europe from the School of the Museum of Fine Arts; $500.- award in Annual Pepsi-Cola Exhibit for 1946, $250.- Popular prize in the same Show; John Hay Whitney Fellowship for study in Mexico, 1950 - 1951; International Institute of Education Exchange -Student Fellowship for study in Mexico; Purchase prize, Hunterson Art Center Annual Print Exhibit, New Jersey; Best Lithograph award 1st National Print Exhibit, Silvermine Guild, Connecticut; Best Cover Design from the International Federation of the Press, Paris, France, 1964; Merit Citation, Society of Illustrators National Exhibit, 1964.

COLLECTIONS: Boston Public Library; Smith College Museum of Art; Museum of Modern Art, New York; Atlanta University; Carnegie Institute; Bezalel Museum, Jerusalem; Howard University; Pepsi-Cola Company; Department of Fine Arts, French Government and many private collections.

POSITIONS: Instructor of Painting at Boris Mirski School of Modern Art, Boston, 1945 - 1947; Boston School of the Museum of Fine Arts, 1950; Instructor in Anatomy, Pratt Institute Evening School, 1958; New York City, Board of Education, 1950 - 1964; Assistent Professor, Boston University, 1964 to present.

REMARKS: Listed in Who's Who in American Art.

CHARLES E. YATES

BORN: in Tennessee, 1940

STUDIED: Currently attending University of Pennsylvania Graduate School of Fine Arts on scholarship.

AWARDS: Cleveland Museum School of Art.

EXHIBITED: Brand Library of Art and Music, Glendale, California; Associated Students Lounge, UCLA; Los Feliz Jewish Community Center.

HARTWELL YEARGANS

BORN: in Kansas City, Missouri, 1918

STUDIED: Art Students League 1848 - 1951

EXHIBITED: Atlanta University, Georgia; Committee for Negro in the Arts, Group Shows, 1950, 1951, 1952; Group Show, ACA Gallery, New

York; Group Show, Afro-Arts Bazaar, New York; Two-Man Show, Matrix Gallery, New York; Lower East Side Neighborhood Ass'n. Annual Shows, 1955 - 1959, 1963; Congress of Racial Equality Group Show, New York, Galeria San Miguel, San Miguel de Allende, Mexico; Galeria May Brooks, Mexico City, Mexico; Graphics currently on exhibit at: AAA Gallery, Roko Gallery, Terrain Gallery, New York, Stoneledge Galleries, Connecticut; Galerie Moos, Montreal, Canada.

COLLECTIONS: Mr. James Farmer, New York; Mr. and Mrs. D. Cunningham, Kansas City, Missouri; Mr. and Mrs. John Hood, New York; Mr. and Mrs. James Brade, New York; Mr. and Mrs. Frank Penny, Gales Ferry, Connecticut; and many others.

POSITION: Chairman of Visual Arts Committee of L.E.N.A., 1958, 1959.

PUBLICATIONS: Drawings included in C.N.A. portfolio published in 1952.

PART THREE

THE PICTURES

AMOS, Emma "HARVEST II"

ARNOLD, Ralph: ``UNTITLED''

BIGGERS, John T.: "BROKEN STONE"

BURNETT, Calvin: "THREE CRIPPLED DRUNKS"

BURROUGHS, Margaret "ABSTRACTION"

CADOO, Joyce: "DECLINE AND FALL"

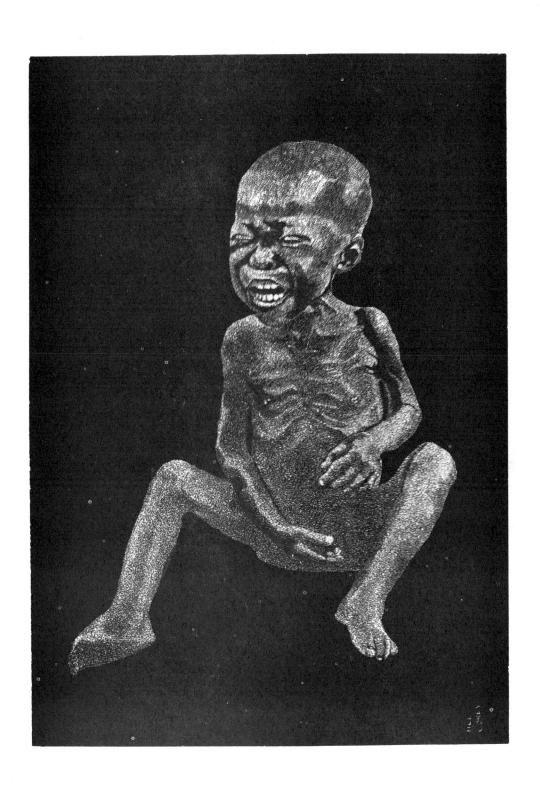

CAREY, Mel: ''HUNGER''

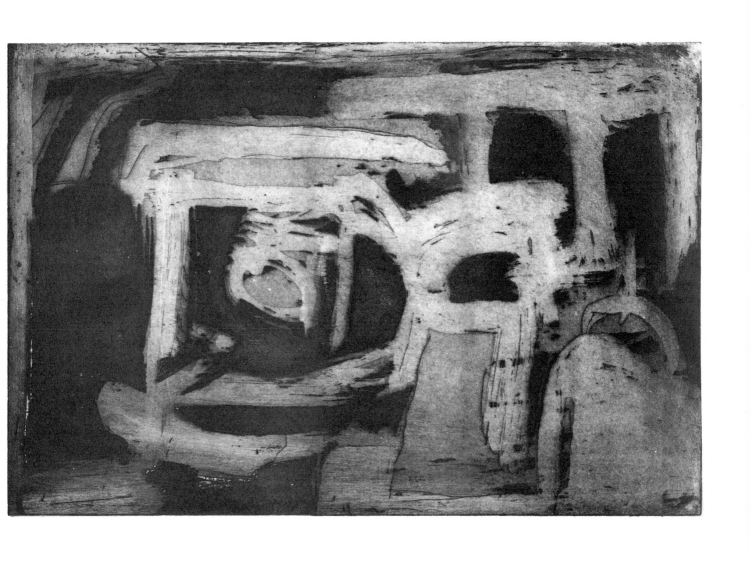

CARTER, Yvonne: ''LATERAL MOVEMENT''

"Roota toot-toot, three times she shot, right through that hotel door"   3/3   Eugene Cheltenham '63

CHELTENHAM, Eugene   "ROOTA TOOT - TOOT....",   Color Woodcut

COLEMAN, Floyd W.: ''IN THE PARK''

COMPTON, Wm. Lawrence: "UNTITLED"

DRISKELL, David C.: "STILL LIFE WITH FRUIT"

DUNN, Eugenia V.: "SHADOWS"

EPTING, Marion A.: "TOTEM"

FERGUSON, Charles: ''UNTITLED''

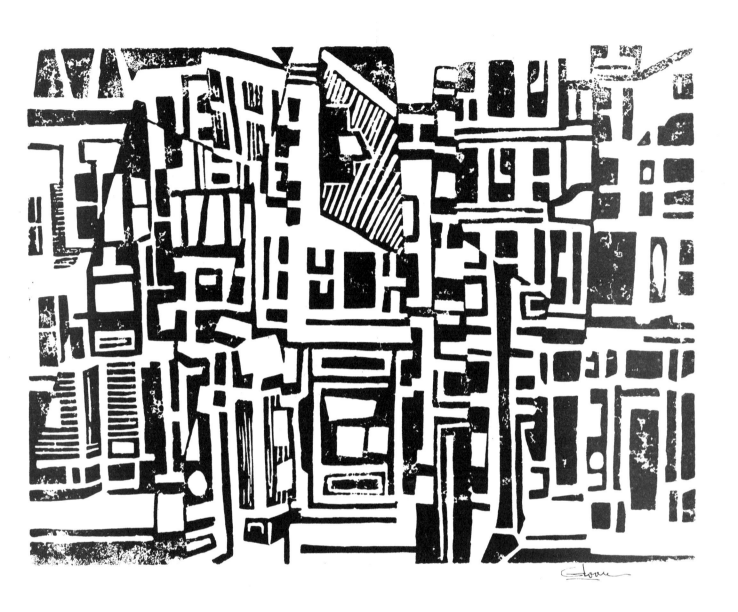

GLOVER, Robert: "CITY"

HARREL, Hugh: "JANIE"

HARRIS, Scotland: ''JAZZ PLAYER''

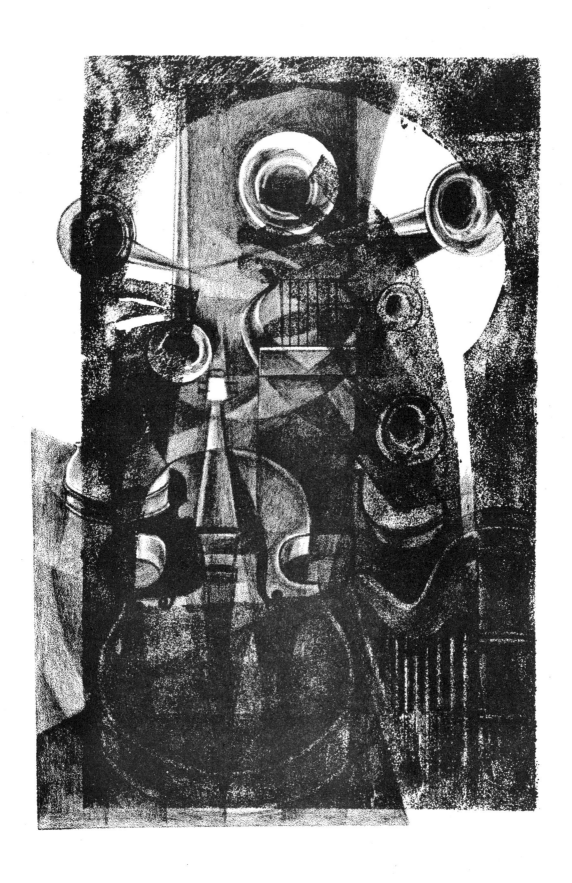

HAWKINS, Eugene: "TAKE NOTE"

HENDERSON, Leroy W.: "LIFT US, WE PRAY"

HICKS, Leon N.: "LITTLE BIRD"

HOLLINGSWORTH, Alvin: "LONELY WOMAN"

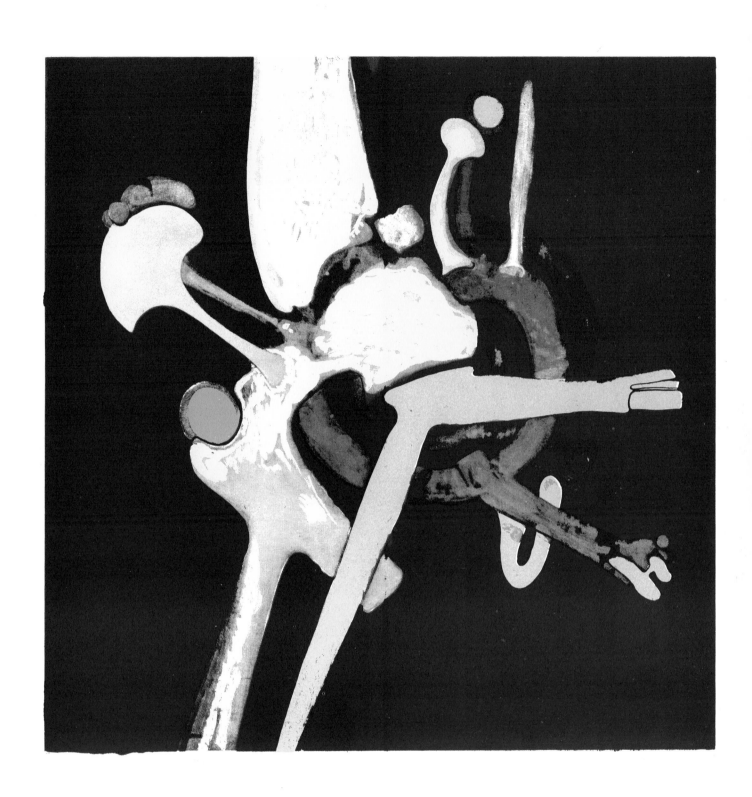

HUNT, Richard: ''UNTITLED''

JAMES, Wilmer: "UNTITLED"

JOHNSON, Milton: "LIMITED"

JORDAN, Jack: GOING HOME

KINNEY, Richard: ''SPRING''

MACKLIN, Anderson: ""AT NOON TIME""

MC CULLOUGH, Geraldine: ""BLACK DIAMOND""

MC NEIL, William: "LIBERA NOS A MALO"

MC NEILL, Lloyd.: "LADY IN LABOR"

MEO, Yvonne: ''STRINGS''

MORGAN, Norma: "DARK HEIGHTS"

MOSELY, Jimmie: "CONTEMPLATION"

PERRY, Michael K.: "TWO FIGURES"

PHILLIPS, Harper T.: "FLIGHT"

POPE, Alvin: "GIRL"

PUSEY, Mavis: "UNTITLED"

PYBURN, Don: MATHEW HENSON

RIDDLE, John: "BILLY RENE"

ROGERS, Charles D.: "AN ADAPTATION FROM THE
THEME OF THE PRODIGAL SON BY MURILLO"

SAAR, Betye "SAMSARA"

'SATCHELL, Ernest: "WORKING IN THE FIELD"

SIMON, Jewel W.: "WALK TOGETHER CHILDREN"

SLATER, Van: "EULA SEATED"

SMITH, Frank E.: ''CITY''

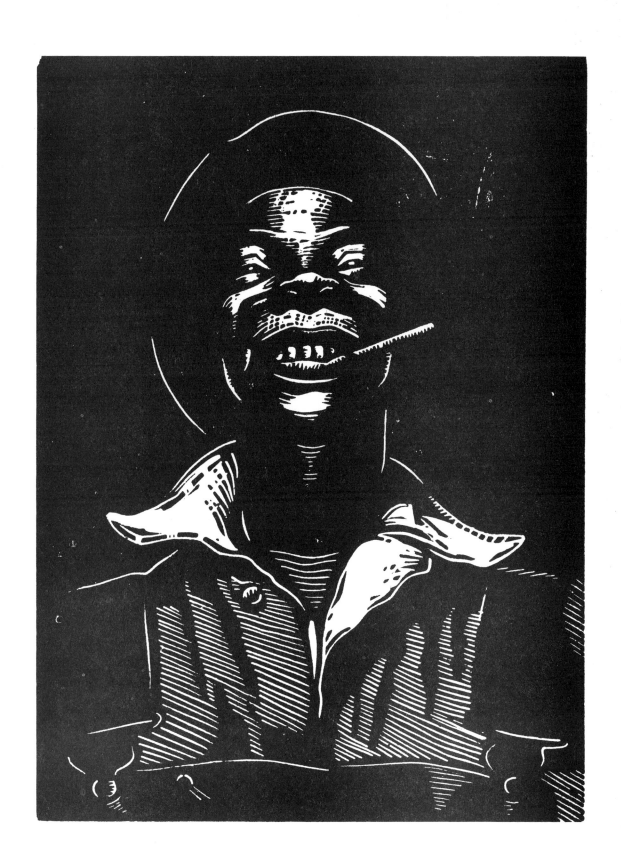

SMITH, William E.: "PAY-DAY"

SMOCK, Sue Jane M.: "PRIESTESS OF OROSUN"

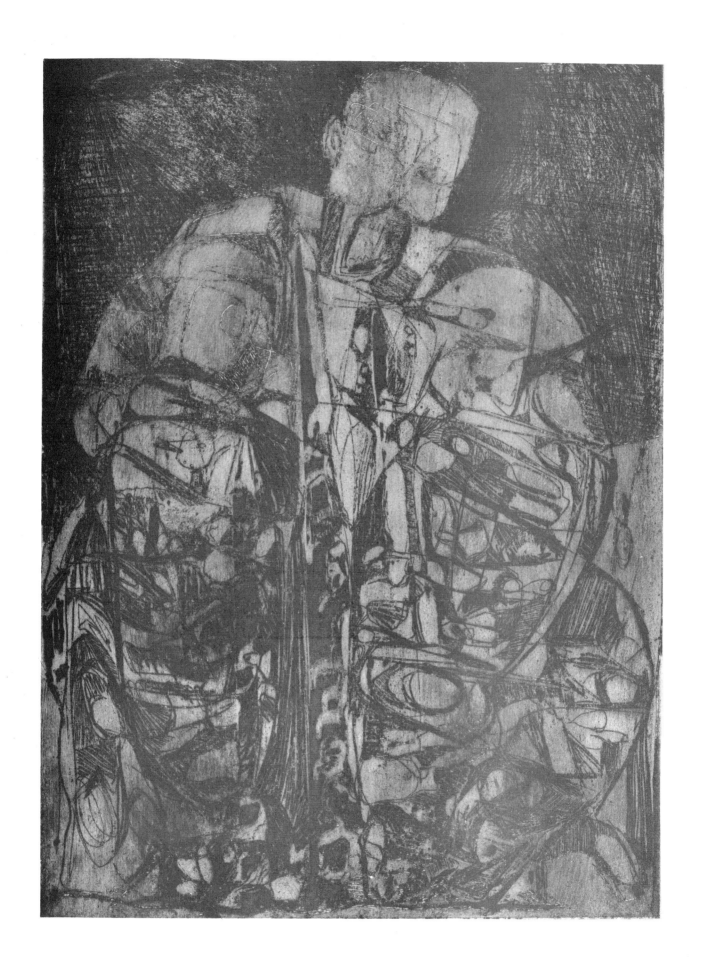

SNOWDEN, Sylvia: "MOUNTAIN MAN"

SOARES, Laura: "SUMMER"

STEPHENS, David F.: "OLIVER G. PERRY"

WADDY, Ruth G.: "MATTER OF OPINION"

WILLIAMS, William: UNTITLED

WILSON, Fred: "THREE IN ONE"

WILSON, John ''LA CALLE''

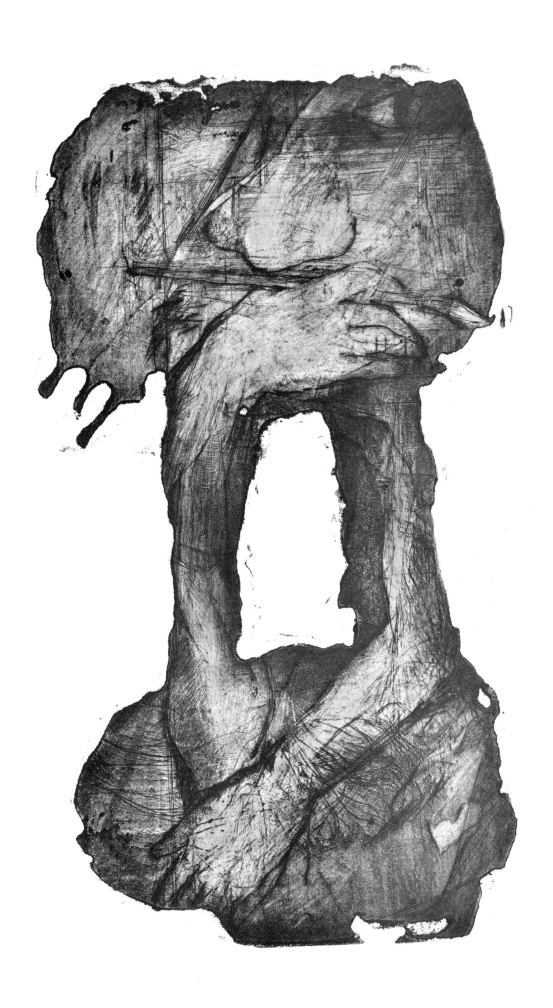

YATES, Charles E.: ''SELF PORTRAIT''

YEARGANS, Hartwell: "FOLKSINGER"